THE QUESTIONS OF JESUS

This book is dedicated to
my Capuchin brothers.
You have been good to me,
and good for me.
Thank you.

Owen O'Sullivan OFM Cap

The Questions
of Jesus

the columba press

First published in 2003 by
the columba press
55A Spruce Avenue, Stillorgan Industrial Park,
Blackrock, Co Dublin

Cover by Bill Bolger
Origination by The Columba Press
The cover picture is from The Last Supper by Giovanni Lanfranco and
is used by permission of The National Gallery of Ireland.
Printed in Ireland by ColourBooks Ltd, Dublin

ISBN 1 85607 423 4

Acknowledgements

The author and publisher gratefully acknowledge the permission of the
following to use material in their copyright: HarperCollins Publishers
Ltd for the Grail version of five verses of Psalm 21; Oneworld
Publications for a quotation from *Rumi: A Spiritual Treasury*. Biblical
quotations are from *The New Revised Standard Version*, copyright 1989
by the Division of Christian Education of the National Council of the
Churches of Christ in the USA. Used by permission. All rights reserved.
Exceptions to the above are: Mark 8:36-37 and John 18:34 are from the
Douai Edition, 1953; Proverbs 27:6 is from the *Jerusalem Bible*, published
and copyright 1966, 1967 and 1968 by Darton, Longman and Todd Ltd
and Doubleday & Co Inc and is used by permission of the publishers.

Contents

Foreword

Christians sometimes go to the bible for answers to questions. And sometimes they come from the bible with questions to answer. God's first question was multi-layered in its significance: 'Where are you?' (Genesis 3:9) The answer was no less so: 'I heard the sound of you in the garden, and I was afraid, because I was naked; and I hid myself.' (3:10) God's questions are probing; our reaction is often to hide, afraid because of our nakedness.

God questioned Job (Job 40:7ff), and the questions led him through a process of reflection to a greater understanding of himself and of God: 'I have uttered what I did not understand, things too wonderful for me, which I did not know … I had heard of you by the hearing of my ear but now my eye sees you.' (Job 42:1-7)

Like Father, like Son. One of the first gospel statements about Jesus is that, at the age of twelve, he was 'in the temple, sitting among the teachers, listening to them and asking them questions.' (Luke 2:46) And he continued doing so: in the New Testament, Jesus posed about one hundred and twenty different questions.

And he asked different types of questions: those which answer a question with a question; those which silence dishonest questioners; those which are a retort. Most can be taken on different levels. The fact that many of the questions are rhetorical enhances their effectiveness in leading us to think, and that is what they are intended to do. They give us the opportunity of entering into a dialogue with Jesus, one in which he takes the lead.

I suggest to the reader to imagine Jesus sitting close by asking these questions, not as an interrogator, but as an intimate and trusted friend, leading us to an understanding of our relationship with God, with others, with ourselves and with nature. The questions of Jesus invite us on a journey of discovery. Their purpose is to bring us to know, accept, and love ourselves as the first step in doing the same towards God and neighbour.

A question such as 'How many loaves have you?' might seem of little significance, the kind of question anyone might ask when going on an outing. But seen in the light of subsequent events it has more meaning; it leads to other questions: 'Why are you talking about having no bread? Do you still not perceive or understand? Are your hearts hardened? Do you have eyes and fail to see? Do you have ears and fail to hear? And do you not remember? When I broke the five loaves for the five thousand, how many baskets full of broken pieces did you collect? And the seven for the four thousand, how many baskets full of broken pieces did you collect? Do you not yet understand?' (Mark 8:17-21) The questions, no less than the teachings of Jesus, formed an interwoven tapestry of meaning that becomes broader and deeper when linked.

There are questions which express Jesus' frustration at his followers' failure to believe. Others, indeed many others, seem intended to wake them up and lead them to alertness.

There are questions which are deeply searching, challenging us to be aware of what is happening in our lives. And we should not be too quick with answers; the true answers come only from life. There are really penetrating questions, such as 'Whom are you looking for?' – one of only two that Jesus asked three times.

And there are the questions Jesus did not ask, like 'What's in it for me?' 'What am I getting out of this?' Their absence speaks for itself.

In presenting the questions I start with the gospel according to Mark, which is seen as a foundational text for the gospels of Matthew and Luke. I took the questions as they appear in Mark's gospel, and then went on to questions from Matthew, Luke, John and Acts which are not found in Mark. The duplication which is found in the four gospels I have avoided in the book. One question – from John 8:25 – I omitted because of the uncertainty of the translation.

My suggestion to the reader is to take one question, that is, one page, at a time, read it once or twice, and then reflect on it for as long as it is helpful. If possible, read the question in its context so as to savour its full meaning. If time allows, read the parallel passages in the other gospels. Give time to it. Reflect quietly. Take no more than one question a day, and use the book for a four-month retreat. Imagine Jesus beside you, asking the question. Then conclude with a period of gentle prayer. My hope is that this process will be for the reader what it was for me, a venture into the interior, a journey of self-discovery, and a greater awareness of the humanity of Jesus.

? *'Why do you raise such questions in your hearts?' (Mark 2:8)*

This is unusual, Jesus. Here you seem not to want people to ask questions, whereas in the rest of the gospel you urge people to think, you challenge them to do it, you even berate them impatiently when they do not think. You did not complain when people questioned you, you welcomed their questions.

Was it the type of questions the scribes were asking that angered you, questions with a negative, even dim-witted character? Were these questioners truly looking for answers, or were they locked in an ideological mould, unable to face reality and draw a conclusion? They seemed to have a frame of mind which was fixated on authority, especially their authority, understood on their terms: if authority said X or Y, then anything which did not fit in with that could not be right, so there was no need to examine it on its merits. What you were doing was outside the framework of their way of thinking, and they choked on it.

The questioners who annoyed you were people who had developed a mental framework for their faith but, in doing so, had slipped into a way of thinking that could not acknowledge another way of looking at things. You were a breaker of moulds, Jesus; you did not have much time for the sort of thinking that would leave people's minds in a safe rut. Your questioners saw themselves as defenders of the faith, the guardians of the tradition. They were not malicious men, just dull, slow in imagination and afraid of risk. Their training had encased them in a mental straitjacket, and they did not even know it. They had ink instead of blood in their veins. When they saw something new, as when you healed the paralytic, they went to their books for an answer. It was not there. The Word was made flesh, but all they knew was words. No wonder you called them blind guides.

Your response to their questions was to create new facts on the ground and let them speak. No one can argue with a fact; it is there whether anyone likes it or not.

You did not get into an argument with them. You responded with a question of your own – which they did not answer. You were patient with most people, Jesus, but you were angered by those who had timidly locked up their minds for fear of something new.

You had a strong personality, Jesus, one not to be trifled with. In effect, you said to your questioners, 'Wake up. Get out of dreamland. Draw the conclusion that is staring you in the face.' You did not have patience, or try to, with those who lived in ivory towers and wanted to stay there.

9

? *'The wedding guests cannot fast, while the bridegroom is still with*
• *them, can they?' (Mark 2:19)*

You were the bridegroom of the image, Jesus, and you enjoyed life. You enjoyed meals: in the gospels you always seem to be either going to a meal, or at a meal, or coming from a meal. You started your public life at a wedding feast and you drew it towards its close at the last supper. You spoke of eternal life with God as a banquet of fine strained wines, and as a marriage supper. You gave your followers a sacred meal as the way to remember you. You were condemned as a glutton and a wine-drinker. Your critics, so prissy and prim, suggested it might have been wiser if you had refrained. They reduced prudence to caution. Did they know what it was to celebrate, to enjoy a good meal, a hearty laugh?

You also enjoyed company, though some said you kept bad company. If we can be judged by the company we keep, then you would be severely judged, as indeed you were. You were told off for associating with women whose reputation preceded them, and people as politically incorrect as tax collectors, those collaborators with foreign rulers, doing their dirty work for them, and making a nice profit on the side. You always had a soft spot for those outside the circle of self-anointed virtue, didn't you?

Your critics should have known better than to be so serious and unsmiling. They came from a tradition which held that, at the end of life, God will call us to account for every pleasure which we did not enjoy. Of course, they trimmed that down by inserting 'legitimate' before 'pleasure'. Adjectives subvert nouns, don't they? You rarely used them. Your critics had a sour and serious religion of inhibitions and prohibitions. What wasn't prescribed was proscribed. The poor, dull plodders, they didn't know what they were missing. What a penny-pinching bore of a God they believed in!

You brought with you something fresh and new, like new wine in new wineskins. Your teaching was new, when all they wanted was that old-time religion; it was good enough for them. You said you came that people might have life and have it to the full. You asked people to take their faith, not themselves, seriously. Is it not true that those religious traditions that frown on the pleasures of food, drink and sex substitute for them the more dangerous pleasures of power? I like what one of your servants wrote,

Where'er the Catholic sun doth shine,
there's music and laughter and good red wine.
At least I have always found it so.
Benedicamus Domino! (Let us bless the Lord.)

10

? *'Have you never read what David did when he and his companions were hungry and in need of food?' (Mark 2:25)*

Necessity knows no law, is that not so, Jesus? David and his companions were hungry, so they went into the temple and ate the loaves offered there each week, loaves which only the priests were allowed to eat. But hunger is a pressing human need, questioned only by the well-fed. If one person's right to the food necessary for life has priority over another person's right to property, then what about the hunger of 800 million people today? Do they not have a right to food, not just a right to beg for it? In our world, one child dies every three seconds of preventable poverty-related illnesses. What an outrage in a world that has more than enough for everyone's need! If I do not feed the hungry, I kill them.

People first, rules second – that was your way. The sabbath was made for the person, not the person for the sabbath. *Mea culpa*, Jesus – because I too have reversed your priorities, following the rules at the expense of the person in the name of obedience or tradition. What crimes have been committed in their name! How often we hide behind them to avoid difficult choices and keep to what is safe and predictable.

Jesus, help me to make the world a better place, better according to your scale of priorities, not mine. It is not unrealistic to hope and work for a world where children do not starve, or die of preventable illnesses. Everyone who has studied this question says it can be done, and done quickly, if there is the will to do it. But it means a change of priorities. I cannot say, as earlier generations might have said with truth, that I did not know about it. I do.

How can I look you in the eye and not be moved at the thought of so much need on the one hand, and so much greed on the other? How is it, Jesus, that warring armies can always be supplied with munitions but, when it comes to feeding the hungry, we hear so much of delays because of logistical problems? How can we human beings be so uncaring? Have mercy on me, Jesus, because I am a part of the problem more than I have been a part of the answer. I use the size of the problem as an excuse for doing nothing. Move me to forget the excuses and to find and take the remedies.

? *'Is it lawful to do good or harm on the sabbath, to save life or to kill?'*
• *(Mark 3:4)*

Surely the answer to your question, Jesus, is self-evident. Of course, it is lawful to do good on the sabbath and to save life, not to do harm or to kill. Once the question is put in that way, there is only one answer that any person can give.

The problem was that the people you were talking to did not see it like that. Their minds were locked into a system of thought they had created, and they were not capable of seeing beyond it. They had reduced religion to a system; their theology had, so to speak, made God redundant. They started off with God as their ruler and ended up with rules as their God. So, when you put the question to them, they remained silent. They had allowed a system of thought, in their case a religious one, to stultify them. It had also corrupted them: they were more interested in scoring a point than in finding the truth.

The gospel says you looked at the people with anger, grieved at their hardness of heart. Lack of respect for truth among those who were meant to be seekers of it by profession was something you could not take. For you, the truth was always something to be further explored, not a sealed package, to be received and handed on.

People who follow an ideology, whether political, economic, scientific or religious, or who obey the dictates of political correctness, make the same mistake as those you questioned. They give it their allegiance, and then stop thinking.

So often, Jesus, you were trying to get people to open their eyes and see, to open their ears and hear, to open their minds and think. Sometimes I let slogans and clichés do my thinking for me. It is a form of laziness, or sometimes moral cowardice.

Give me the courage, Jesus, to be prepared to follow the truth wherever it leads me, one step at a time, not knowing where the next step will lead, for whoever seeks the truth – any truth – seeks you. Give me the breadth of vision to be able to move beyond the safety of where I am, the security of how I think, and the familiarity of what I do. Entrusting myself to you, Jesus, may I, in solidarity with others, launch out into the deep.

? *'How can Satan cast out Satan?' (Mark 3:23)*

Jesus, you spoke of the divided self, of people who have a civil war raging within them. That is most of us, isn't it? We have in us the division between *is* and *ought*, between *what I am* and *what I could be*.

You spoke with that mixture of sadness and anger that came to you when you saw people playing devious, cunning, petty games with the true and the good. When they saw you do good, they attributed it to Satan. When you spoke a truth they did not want to hear, they indulged in word games and niggling arguments. It was then you spoke some of the most terrible words in the gospel: 'Whoever blasphemes against the Holy Spirit can never have forgiveness, but is guilty of an eternal sin.' (Mark 3:29)

What is that blasphemy? I believe it is to deny the truth, to belittle the good, and to spit on beauty. If that becomes a habit, there develops a depth of corruption that is beyond remedy, unless the person is broken down, utterly smashed and beaten. (Maybe that accounts for the violence of your language against the Pharisees.) Then there is the possibility of regeneration – a hope, no more.

Let me never give way to cynicism, Jesus. When I am cynical, I deny it: I say I am being realistic. I point the finger of blame at those I hold responsible, but the other three fingers point back to myself.

Cynicism is the bastard brother of despair. There is no good that it cannot destroy. It is a cancer, drawing vitality from its host and killing it. May I not try to present tiredness, negativity or pessimism as evidence of wisdom, experience or maturity. May I not use the wisecrack to raise a laugh while doing a demolition job on someone's hopes or ideals, even if they were naïve or simplistic. Save me from that unclean spirit, Jesus.

? *'Who are my mother and my brothers?' (Mark 3:33)*

Your parents and relatives did not understand you, Jesus, not even when you were a child. And when you were grown up, they went out to restrain you because they thought you were out of your mind. They believed they were doing it for your own good. I can sense their frustration: 'Why can't he be normal, like everyone else?' I can hear them advising you, 'Whatever you say, say nothing.' They were there, anxiously nudging you to do what they thought you should be doing, so that you had to rebuke even your mother. Her mother love could have become smother love, and you would not allow anyone to cling to you. If you had done what they wanted, you would, of course, not have been crucified – but neither would you have saved humanity.

There is an arrogance in me, Jesus, when I presume that I understand another person, and assume a right to decide on their behalf. How can I think that, when I am a mystery even to myself? If I cannot understand myself, how can I presume to lay claim to knowledge of another?

The ones who understood you, even if in muddled fashion, were your followers, not only those around you in your homeland at that time, but anyone who does the will of your Father today or at any time in any place.

What is it to do the will of your Father? Even Peter, not the brightest of your followers, came to see that in every nation anyone who fears God and does what is right is acceptable to him. What is it to do what is right? It is to recognise and respect the humanity of the other.

I am thinking of the politician who stands up for the rights of his opponent, the trade unionist who risks death by defending workers' rights, the journalist who risks ostracism by being politically incorrect, the human rights worker who refuses to be intimidated by power-groups, or the ecologist who plants a tree in an industrial slum, knowing it may be vandalised the next day. I am thinking of all those people who care for someone other than themselves. If we do what is right by people, then by God we're not wrong.

Jesus, you asked for total commitment. You said, in effect, that I should let nothing and no one stand in the way of doing your Father's will. Most of the time it is myself.

Jesus, help me to love God our Father as you loved him – unconditionally. And then I will love others as I ought.

? *'Do you not understand this parable? Then how will you understand all the parables?' (Mark 4:13)*

You taught in parables, Jesus. Not for you the abstract propositions of Greek philosophy. When asked who was a neighbour, you did not enunciate a definition of the term neighbour, you told the parable of the good Samaritan.

Your parables are like mirrors held up to life in which we see the truth about ourselves. Who do we identify with in the parable? – that is the question. Your parables are gentle traps. Their method is to lead me to concede a point which I had not considered as applicable to myself, and also to see that the scope of the answer is broader than I had thought.

The parables have a sense of urgency about them. It was as if you knew that, given half a chance, we would wriggle off the hook and avoid drawing out the implications of the story. Pretend you don't understand and ask for clarification – that is our way of dodging it - anything to avoid commitment. But you want us, not just to think clearly, but to act decisively, and you use the parables as a prod to bring that about. They show how well you knew people.

Your way of teaching teaches me about you, Jesus. There was nothing pedantic about you, nothing hectoring or talking down. Some teachers would bore a woodworm to death, but you draw your hearers into the process. You lead us to reflect on a situation you describe and, from there, to reflect on ourselves. You create images more than words, you draw pictures in our heads. The pictures show your interest in people, an interest which is spiced with a humour that is sympathetic but unsentimental. They leave us with questions to answer about ourselves. You do not spell out the answer for us, but trust to our intelligence to work the answer out for ourselves. You do not go in for spoon feeding, spelling out answers in words of one syllable for us when we are too lazy to think.

The response that I give to your parables is what makes me an insider or an outsider. I learn more about the bible from trying to live it than from studying it, and I become an insider or an outsider in relation to your rule by responding or not to your parables. Thank you, Jesus, for your parables. They are an endless source of reflection and a vigorous stimulus to action.

? *'Is a lamp brought in to be put under the bushel basket, or under the bed, and not on the lampstand?' (Mark 4:21)*

Your question, Jesus, is rhetorical. The answer is self-evident. In your country at your time, lights were precious. Fuel was expensive and, if people could afford it, they did not waste it, they made the most of it. I remember a young man in Madagascar whom I asked about what his family did in the evening when the sun set. I knew they did not have lights: electricity did not exist in rural areas and fuel was beyond the reach of their pocket. He said, 'We sang.' No wonder they are a nation of singers, who can harmonise without rehearsal, and do so beautifully for any and every occasion.

I remember the people on the border between Angola and Zambia who told me how they could see the fires of their village in the distance, across the plain in the evening, when they made the long journey back home from the sugar-fields in the south at the end of the cutting season. Like beacons, the light of the fires guided them home.

The whole point of a light is to give of itself; that is its reason for existence, it literally burns itself out. In that respect it is like love, living in order to give. And even the smallest light can penetrate the darkest dark; a small stump of a candle can give as much light as a large new one. And the light of a candle enlightens everyone in the room; it does not illuminate selectively. It also gives warmth, maybe only a little, but a lot of light with a little added warmth does much good. How true that it is better to light a candle than to curse the dark!

There is a warning, too. Any candle – even a blessed one – can burn. The truth, even a 'small' truth, if there is such a thing, is not to be trifled with. It is not a toy for us to play with, but a gift to be respected, accepted gratefully as something given.

On Holy Saturday night, when the Easter candle is brought into the darkened church, the people light their candles from it, the one candle giving birth to many lights; the candle, symbolising you, Jesus, the light of the world, giving its light until the whole church glows with yellow lights and illuminated faces, a parable in action. The dispersal of the light does not dim the Easter candle, it can go on forever giving more and more light, endlessly. You said, 'I am the light of the world. Whoever follows me will never walk in darkness but will have the light of life.' The best way to keep the faith is to share it.

? *'Why are you afraid? Have you still no faith?' (Mark 4:40)*

Jesus, I once counted the number of times you said, 'Fear not'. It was eighty-three, many of them in the gospel of your servant Mark. I may have missed some but still, eighty-three times is enough for me to get the message: you do not want me to be afraid.

Why is this so important to you? I think it may be that fear clouds the truth, especially the truth about myself. Fear constricts, narrows, blinds the vision, paralyses action. Much of what we do in life is a matter of running away from ourselves; we plunge into substitutes to avoid looking ourselves in the face. But you want us to look ourselves and reality in the face, since self-knowledge is the beginning of spiritual growth. If I know myself then I have already begun to know you.

Most people are afraid, for example, afraid that if others knew the truth about them, they would not like them. But what is our greatest fear? I think it is of love, intimacy and commitment. We fear them, believing they entail a loss of freedom. But without them there is no belonging; life becomes a series of experiments, a merciless sequence of choices leading to desolation of spirit. It becomes a matter of living in the land of perpetual postponement, skimming over the surface of everything, and never living in depth. Having no commitment to another means living within the boundaries of the self, never truly reaching out or growing beyond its narrow limitations.

You ask if I have still no faith? I can answer, Jesus, with the man in the gospel: 'I believe, Lord, help my unbelief.' I believe, but my belief is weak. Strengthen it, Jesus.

You link my fear to my lack of faith. If I had greater faith in you, I would not be afraid to take the plunge of commitment. I would not hedge my bets. I would give you everything in one great generous gift and not call it back. If my faith were stronger I would see that all things are in your hands, that everything is connected to everything else, the whole of reality is interdependent, each part like a note harmonised into one symphony of which you are the sound. There is no DIY spirituality, and the Lone Ranger is a model of nothing but despair. We humans need each other if we are to live humanly. Fear is the product of self-love, so you taught that 'Perfect love casts out fear.'

? *'What is your name?' (Mark 5:9)*

You already know my name, Jesus, you are not looking for missing information. You said to me, 'I have called you by name and you are mine.' My identity is no secret to you.

A name is not reducible to a tag for calling someone; it is a summary of an individual's personality and character. Your own name – Jesus – means 'God is salvation'. Your question means, 'Who are you? What kind of person are you? Do you know yourself?' To know a name is to have power over what it signifies. You gave Abram the name of Abraham, Simon you called Peter, and Saul became Paul, each receiving a new mission with his name.

You first put your question to a man possessed by demons, and his answer was, 'My name is Legion; for we are many.' This was ambiguous: 'legion' could mean 6,000 soldiers considered as a unit, or 6,000 individuals. No straight answers to straight questions, the evasion of truth, a sign of the presence of evil. And yet his failure to give a straight answer betrayed the truth, despite himself: his was a divided self.

You call us to unity, to integrity; holiness is wholeness. You spoke of reconciliation – we need it with ourselves. Atonement means at-one-ment – the state of being at one, at one with the self in the first place. This means dropping the masks I hide behind, and thereby putting myself at risk. It means letting go of attempts to impose on my actual self the image of the ideal self that I think I ought to be. It means accepting myself as I am, saying, 'By the grace of God I am what I am.' If I can say that and mean it, then by the grace of God I will become what I can become. If I accept myself and am at peace with myself, then I will accept others and be at peace with them. I see others as I see myself; I see what is within me.

Jesus, you said, 'Blessed are the pure in heart, for theirs is the kingdom of heaven.' I believe you meant by that, 'Blessed are the single-minded, those of undivided heart, those who give an unambiguous answer.' You love those whose yes means yes, whose no means no. They were free people, free to love with totality. You love those who give themselves with full commitment to a person or an ideal, and who persevere in that commitment through thick and thin, the good times and the bad, in sickness and in health until death does them part.

May I hold fast to your name. To those who do, you promised to give a white stone with a new name written on it which is known to no one except the one who receives it. That new name, with all its meaning and significance, is the entry into new life with you.

? *'Why do you make a commotion and weep?' (Mark 5:39)*

This evokes memories of Africa for me, too many to recount. People, especially women, would indeed 'make a commotion and weep' at funerals. At one such, I was surprised to see a woman whom I knew well, a primary school teacher, become seemingly hysterical at the funeral of someone who was a relative stranger to the area. On the way home afterwards, I asked her if she was related to the dead person. She replied to my question with one of her own, 'Do you think that because I cried so much?' I said 'Yes.' She responded simply, 'It is expected of us.' And the same used to be true in Ireland, the professional keeners making sure the deceased had a good send-off with lots of keening and moaning.

At times I used to find the ritualistic, formalised weeping an irritation; at other times, I was tempted to laugh, especially if the performance seemed particularly melodramatic. In one place they really went over the top, throwing handfuls of dust in the air, and banging their heads off the (straw!) walls of a hut, before making the discovery that the body brought to the village for burial was the wrong one! Before beginning funeral prayers, I used to ask for silence, and often noticed that the loud wailing would be switched off like a light. I felt like saying, 'Let's bring a bit of dignity into the proceedings.'

I think, Jesus, that maybe you felt the same on this occasion when you went to the house of the synagogue leader whose daughter had died. You cleared them all out of the house, except for your three chosen companions. After all, you needed space and air to breathe in a stifling room. I understand fully, I would have done the same myself.

You said, 'Do not fear, only believe', almost the same as before. And you raised the dead girl to life.

In your sight, death is of no consequence. To us it matters a great deal, to you not at all. We remain safe in your hands; with death our life has changed, not ended. A believer can look death in the eye and not be troubled by it, like Saint Francis of Assisi who said, 'Welcome, Sister Death.'

? *'How many loaves have you?' (Mark 6:38)*

Some of your questions, Jesus, like this one, seem to be on a simple, factual level – the kind of question anyone might ask when going on a journey. But even this question has more meaning when seen in the light of subsequent events.

You were often impatient with your followers, Jesus. You were constantly giving them wake-up calls, and they, almost as constantly, missed the point. But they were not tame or passive. A moment before, they had asked you, 'Are we to go and buy two hundred denarii worth of bread, and give it to them to eat?' I find it hard not to see that question as sarcastic: they must have known there was nowhere to buy bread in a place three times described as 'deserted'. Or perhaps they meant: 'Do you think we are made of money, that we have two hundred days' wages jingling in our pockets to spend on this lot?'

Your relationship with your followers, Jesus, was not easy. You got on each others' nerves. Strong personalities, uprooted from their ordinary environment, you knocked sparks off each other. Communication between you was real and to the point, sometimes blunt.

Maybe that was what made a team of them, creating the mutual loyalty that enabled Simon the Jewish nationalist to resist the temptation to knife Matthew the tax-collector, the collaborator with the Roman imperial power.

James and John you nick-named 'sons of thunder' because of their fiery temper when they felt slighted.

Peter was emotional and changeable. One moment he proclaimed his faith in you, in the next he misunderstood you. His heart was in the right place but he was not very reliable, was he?

Philip was a cheerful cynic: 'Nazareth? Can anything good come from that place?' He did not understand you, even later on, asking you to show them the Father and then they would be satisfied.

Thomas the doubter, the skeptic, must have been hard to put up with. But his doubt confirms our faith.

And then, of course, there was Judas, who sold you for the price of a slave.

The rest of the Twelve were also rans, so obscure we are not sure even of their names.

All in all, Jesus, not an impressive selection, not the cream of the crop – just like ourselves, in fact. But they were the ones you chose. They became the founders of your community of faith. So maybe there is hope for the rest of us.

? *'Do you also fail to understand? Do you not see that whatever goes into a person from the outside cannot defile, since it enters, not the heart but the stomach, and goes out into the sewer?' (Mark 7:18-19)*

Jesus, you were trying to open the minds of those zealous but narrow people who were concerned about the minutiae of religious observance. They knew of foods which were forbidden and those which were not, what kinds of social contact defiled people, rendering them ritually impure and therefore unfit for temple worship, what work was permitted or forbidden on the sabbath. They wrote tomes filled with these intricate details, so many that a person could hardly read them all, much less remember or observe them.

Yes, Jesus, we are the same. We are so careful about the trivialities, for instance, the details of social etiquette, dressing in the right way, knowing which cutlery to use at a feast, being fluent in the right forms of address to local dignitaries, being able to talk knowledgeably about wines, observing the canons of political correctness, being deferential to the powerful, making sure to smile at the rich even if the smile is as unreal as an advertisement for toothpaste. We do these things because we are afraid of each other, afraid of what others might think.

These rules and rituals of exclusion upend priorities. The guards in the Nazi death camps went home from the daily routine of mechanised murder to listen to classical music, go to the theatre, visit friends and engage in social chit-chat. A mother urges her pregnant teenage daughter to – for heaven's sake! – think of the family name and have an abortion. The businessman who is a pillar of rectitude in the local community may have made his money from sweat-shop labour in the Third World.

It is what comes out of a person that defiles. For it is from within, from the human heart that evil intentions come: fornication, theft, murder, adultery, avarice, wickedness, deceit, licentiousness, envy, slander, pride, folly. All these evil things come from within, and they defile a person.

What troubled you about sin, Jesus, is not the offence it causes God, who is beyond our offending anyway, but the harm it does to us.

21

? *'Why does this generation ask for a sign?' (Mark 8:12)*

It is true, Jesus. We look for a sign, for something spectacular, something dramatic to demonstrate your power, to establish who you are. Like your followers, who kept asking you for a sign to vindicate your claim to authority, we want to reduce you to a performer, a magician who will perform tricks at our bidding. And you did not do that for anyone. You sighed deeply in your spirit and said, 'Truly, I tell you, no sign will be given to this generation.'

Of course, the signs were there, and are there, if we have eyes open to see them. We would like you to turn water into wine as you did at Cana, but we fail to see it happening all the time in vineyards. I remember my first time seeing vines in winter. They looked dead, fit only to be uprooted and used for firewood. The ground was hard, dry and chalky. You could hardly imagine a less likely setting for the growth of bunches of fat, juicy grapes. But a few months later the vines were heavy with fruit and it was time for the vintage.

A farmer sows a seed in the ground, covers it over, then leaves it and goes on to the next one. Some time later the seed breaks open in the soil and begins to germinate. Rain falls, sun shines and a plant begins to take life. It send out shoots, grows, blossoms, bears fruit and produces new seeds for the next generation. I once saw bamboo, thick as a person's arm, grow at the rate of a hand's length each day. I took photos of it for seven days in succession with a person standing alongside it to illustrate its growth.

If these things happened only once we would call them miracles. But they happen all the time, so we call them natural – and take them for granted. People who live beside the great natural wonders of the world are puzzled as to why tourists come from the ends of the earth to see them.

The signs you give us do not compel assent; they elicit faith in those who have not shut their minds against it. From the greatness and beauty of created things comes a corresponding perception of their Creator. Sometimes I put you to the test, Jesus, and want you to come on my terms, in my way, within the framework of whatever mental categories I am working with at the moment. But you said, 'Do not put the Lord your God to the test.' Forgive my arrogance, Jesus, and open my mind to see what is before me.

? *'Why are you talking about having no bread? Do you still not perceive or understand? Are your hearts hardened? Do you have eyes and fail to see? Do you have ears and fail to hear?' And do you not remember? When I broke the five loaves for the five thousand, how many baskets full of broken pieces did you collect? Do you not yet understand?' (Mark 8:17-21)*

That was quite a blast, Jesus! But I deserve it. Like the rest of humanity, I am sleep-walking through life, day-dreaming, unthinking and unaware.

Do I not perceive? I perceive that if children are not trained and taught they will not learn, that without ideals, direction and leadership they will go astray, but I do not want to get involved. I leave it to their mother, or I say 'That is what schools are for.'

Is my heart hardened? Eighty per cent of sickness and disease in the Third World is caused by lack of access to clean water and sanitation, and every eight seconds a child dies because of a water-related disease. But that still does not move me to a change of lifestyle, to spend less on drink, entertainment, cosmetics and pet food. Yes, Jesus, I have eyes and fail to see, ears and fail to hear.

Do I have eyes and fail to see, and ears and fail to hear? When nuclear war threatened between India and Pakistan, and an Indian army general said that his country could afford to lose twenty-five million people, the whole world should have screamed 'Stop!' in outrage. But we said and did nothing. Why? Well, there was a row on between a footballer and the team manager. And after that, there was the soccer World Cup, so you see … Yes, Jesus, I have eyes and fail to see, ears and fail to hear.

Do I not remember? Yes, Jesus, I remember that nearly every war fought since the Industrial Revolution has been lost by the country which started it. I also know that the political institutions which should deal with injustice are ineffective, so people take up war in desperation. But war creates war. I remember that humanity – and that includes me – is in a special class of slow learners. All those lessons later, and I still have not got the message; I am still cheering on my side.

Do I not yet understand? I understand that we become like those we hate, yet I indulge anger and unforgiveness. I still insist that some row or other was a matter of principle, though I know it was a matter of pride. Jesus, how truly you said, 'Father, forgive them for they know not what they do.'

? *'Can you see anything?' (Mark 8:23)*

There is more than one kind of seeing, Jesus, isn't there?

There is seeing with the eyes of the body, the two you gave me that enable me to know colour, shape and size. Thank you, Jesus, for the gift of sight. I never notice the water until the well runs dry, and I will never fully appreciate the gift of sight unless I lose it. Thank you, again.

There is seeing with the eyes of the mind, being mentally alive and alert, awake and active. Jesus, help me to keep my mind alive. Do not let it grow stale through laziness. Do not let me fall into the trap of going with the flow or, out of cowardice, suppressing what I believe. You gave me a mind so that I would use it. You do not want me to be a parrot.

There is seeing with the eyes of the soul, being perceptive, able to read between the lines, being spiritually attuned, able to see below the surface of things, able to read the signs of the times. Enable me, Jesus, to welcome truth wherever I find it, whether it is in the action of a prophet, the song of a pop-star, the wisdom of a philosopher, the rhythm of a poet, the suffering of the sick, the silent beauty of nature, or the innocence of a child. 'Whoever is not against you is for you.' All truth is God's truth.

I know that this seeing with the eyes of the soul is a gradual process, Jesus, and I do not expect it to come this minute. But may I play my part, by opening my eyes and looking at what is in front of me. May I recognise reality as it is, and call it by name. Let me not live in a dream-world of make-believe, seeing only what I want to see and turning away from what I do not want to see. May I not mutilate the truth by denying or misnaming it. May I accept that the truth is not for me to possess, but something by which I am to be possessed. No truth is ever 'mine'; it is always yours. May I accept that to arrive at belief I must pass through doubt. May I not seek a short cut that bypasses that process. If I play my part, you will play yours.

? *'Who do people say that I am?' (Mark 8:27)*

Some say you are a great teacher, a moral philosopher. But what teacher was ever so arrogant as to say, not merely 'I teach the truth', but, as if that were not arrogant enough, 'I am the truth'?

Some say you are the great pioneering social worker because you pointed the way to solving problems, you cared for the needy, you healed, you lifted up the down-trodden, you fed, you even raised the dead to life. But that was not why you died on a cross, Jesus, was it?

Some see you, though they do not put it so bluntly, as the cosmic Santa Claus, who gives gifts to those who ask, the great soother who anaesthetises us from the harshness of reality, the celestial comforter who gives us a cuddle and a kiss and puts us to sleep.

Some say you are the cause – the unwitting cause but the cause nonetheless – of wars, persecutions and religious divisions. You are the well-meaning man who got carried away by his greatness and his gifts, and exalted himself to the level of divinity. You are the one who forgot the lesson of the temptations in the desert and succumbed to the lure of power, seduced by the notion of being the saviour of the world.

Some say the world would have been a better place if you had never been born, that the talk of your being a redeemer takes from people a sense of responsibility for themselves, allowing them to off-load it onto you, and that this keeps them in a state of spiritual childishness which they will never outgrow as long as they look to you as their saviour. They say we can achieve our potential only when we stand erect, in solidarity with others, facing the world and its terrors with our unaided strength, and that this is the truth which redeems and saves.

Some say you showed us a process of discovery about the self, about others, nature and God, a process gradually obscured through the centuries, becoming instead a structure of power and control, the very thing from which you had sought to free your people. We need to let go the institution and re-discover the process, they say. Then Jesus will have fulfilled his mission.

Some say that you are the Metaphysical Ground of our Being. Sorry, Jesus, I kept the worst news till last; I could not bear to start with that one.

? *'But who do you say that I am?'* (Mark 8:29)

Maybe this is the most difficult of all your questions, Jesus. If not, then it is the second most difficult. I know you do not want a text-book answer taken from a creed or a catechism. That sort of answer would evoke from you another of your questions: 'Do you say this of yourself or have others told you of me?' You are asking me what I think, and that does not leave me any wriggle room. You expect a straight answer to a straight question, and you are entitled to it.

You have been different things to me at different times of my life. In my student days I was offered a dose of saccharine sweet Jesus, meek and mild, tame and toothless as a child. It was a distraction; I hope my present understanding is closer to the gospel.

I like your humour; you had a gently irony. I like your emotional warmth, especially your anger at hypocrisy, at institutions placing themselves above people, at people in power hiding behind systems, and your frustration at the stupidity of your followers. These find an echo in me.

I like the way you championed the underdogs without sentimentalising them: 'Stand up, take your mat and walk,' you said to the man who had a touch of self-pity in his complaint that no one would help him. I like your earthy realism about people: 'You are looking for me because you ate your fill of the loaves.' I like the way you challenged people, combining mercy and truth: 'Go your way, and from now on do not sin again.'

I like your ability to break out of the mental limits of the religion, customs and culture of your time and place, reaching beyond the local to the universal: 'There were many lepers in Israel at the time of the prophet Elisha, and none of them was cleansed except Naaman the Syrian.'

I like the priority you gave to the truth, regardless of the risk, as when you told your followers things they did not want to hear. I like your ability to unmask the deviousness of the disingenuous, like those who would not answer a straight question; I like the way you dislodged them from their pretentious perch.

There is so much that I like in you, Jesus, and there is always more to discover. May I never sit in comfort with 'my' Jesus, my private idol. May you comfort me when I am afflicted and afflict me when I am comfortable. Lead me always on, always restless, always questioning, discovering and re-discovering, because all truth is yours, and when I search for the truth I search for you, and you have said, 'Search and you will find.'

? *'What shall it profit a man if he gain the whole world, and suffer the loss of his soul? Or what can a man give in exchange for his soul?'*
(Mark 8:36-37, Douai version)

You are asking me, Jesus, about my priorities. It is not too difficult to know what they are: all I have to do is look at how I spend my time and money.

Is my life self-centred, self-sufficient, self-satisfied or just plain selfish? That is one of the risks of being celibate. Without marriage and family life it is easy to close in on oneself, to allow the great devouring Ego, the almighty I, the magnetic Me, to become an unholy trinity, to swallow up interest or concern for anyone else. Is there any life more wasted than a self-centred one? I cannot think of any.

'You have made us for yourself, Lord, and our hearts will know no rest until they rest in you,' said Saint Augustine. He was right. Without being centred on you, there is no centre that satisfies, just ersatz substitutes, such as addictions, that leave us tired and empty. We were made for greatness; to ignore you is to settle for pettiness. We were made for the fullness of justice, truth and freedom; without you all we have are our helpless, inadequate attempts. We were made for joy and happiness; in the isolation of pretended independence there is only a joyless grey, without colour, laughter or music. We were made for what is genuine; apart from you we have only the trivial and the second-rate.

We were made for others; to live for the self is the ultimate betrayal. Hell is knowing that I was made for others, especially the Other, but that I have instead chosen the narrowness of the self.

You said it, Jesus, 'Those who want to save their life will lose it, and those who lose their life for my sake, and for the sake of the gospel, will save it.' A logician would not be happy with that statement, but it is true all the same. The experience of life bears it out. The happiest people I have known are those who think of others and care for them, and the unhappiest are those who are self-absorbed. The gospel is full of your paradoxes, Jesus, those apparent contradictions that reveal the truth to anyone who looks for their meaning. There is no self-fulfilment without self-denial.

Jesus, do not let me be drawn down into the destructive whirlpool of self-centredness; raise me up into the fountain of self-giving. May I live for you.

? *'How then is it written about the Son of Man, that he is to go through many sufferings and be treated with contempt?' (Mark 9:12)*

It was about yourself, Jesus, that you spoke. You were the Son of Man who was to go through many sufferings. That was your way; you chose it. When you were tempted by Satan in the desert to walk the way of power, you rejected it.

Imagine what it would be like if you had consented. If you had turned bread into stones, you would surely have won a following. You knew that; you said to the people that they were with you because they ate their fill of the loaves. And if you had thrown yourself from the pinnacle of the temple, only to be rescued by angels, that would have been just the kind of display to bring a crowd. And if you had adored Satan, what then? He had promised to give you all the kingdoms of the world if you did so, but were they his to give? He is the father of lies. Had you bent the knee, there would have been no gift of kingdoms, only hollow, mocking laughter resounding through a despairing universe. Satan said in effect, 'Renounce your humanity; it is a limitation unworthy of you. Assert your divinity, with all its power. That is what will win you a following.' And you said no.

You consciously chose a way other than that of power. You chose the way of suffering and weakness. You were God-made-suffering, God-made-weak and contemptible, the ultimate paradox – God in pain. Only a God of love could have conceived such a plan. Is there any greater evidence of God's love than his willingness to enter into the human condition with all its weakness, pain, limitation and suffering?

We, your followers, have been unwilling to follow your example. History is full of our deviation from your chosen path, seeking instead to play the power game, to ingratiate ourselves with the high and mighty, to seek and love titles, honours and positions. We create structures that are not gospel-serving nor people-serving, but self-serving and power-serving. We let ourselves believe that it is all for the good of the cause. But power-seeking levies its taxes: the weak are walked on, truth is manipulated, freedom subverted, justice sold short, the individual crushed.

Whenever your followers have chosen the path of power, you have sent persecutions to return us to your path. I cannot ask to enjoy persecution; I am not brave enough for that. Grant me instead to accept the truth you sought to teach us when you renounced power and chose suffering, the way of humanity.

? *'What are you arguing about with them?' (Mark 9:16)*

Jesus, your followers had got into an argument with some scribes. It was not for the first time nor the last, and they did not resolve anything. Arguments don't usually, do they?

Many of us know how to argue but not how to dialogue. On radio or TV people often do not listen to each other; they interrupt one another, or do not address the issue, or try to score points with cheap shots.

Argument or debate is about coming out on top, silencing your opponent, and being able to say, 'I won.' The person who argues may win the debate, but lose the truth, so what has been gained? In argument, truth is often an early casualty, with justice and courtesy following soon after. Argument works on the principle of 'an eye for an eye', and it makes the whole world blind. Those who shout get shouted at. Argument divides people, it hardens positions and makes listening less likely. People dig themselves into trenches. Argument often evokes anger, and increases the difficulty of creating an atmosphere receptive of truth.

Argument sometimes involves posturing and bluffing, but people see through that, so the one who argues loses credibility, and people then take what he says with a grain of salt. This could be to his loss when he has a genuine case and is hoping for support. He may fail to get it because he is seen as a grandstander playing to a gallery. Argument muddies relationships and makes people less receptive to one's point of view.

Dialogue is about listening, about trying to find what is true, just, or good in the other's position. It means seeing the other as a fellow human being rather than as an opponent. It requires clarity of expression, and a refusal to be drawn into the use of personal attack or offensive bitterness. It distinguishes policies and personalities. It recognises that we have something to learn from the other. It knows that those who listen are likely to be listened to. Dialogue recognises that communication is more about the ears and the heart than the mouth and the mind. It unites people and makes friends. Argument creates confrontation; dialogue builds cooperation.

Thank you, Jesus, for making me stop and think.

? *'You faithless generation, how much longer must I be with you?*
• *How much longer must I put up with you?' (Mark 9:19)*

How often you said things like this to your followers, Jesus, and to me also! They had tried but failed to drive a harmful spirit out of a boy. You asked the boy's father how long it had been happening. He answered, 'From childhood,' and went on to say, 'If you are able to do anything, have pity on us and help us.' Your response was to take up what he had just said, 'If you are able! – All things can be done for the one who believes.' Then the boy's father spoke those honest, heartfelt words, 'I believe; help my unbelief!'

I love those words of his. He spoke for me and for many, perhaps for all of humanity when he said them. I believe, I want to believe, and I live with doubts. But I do not think that doubt is the opposite of belief. It is its necessary partner, the pole which complements it. 'We come to the house of faith only after we have travelled through the forest of doubt,' said one of your servants.

You gave us a mind to think with, Jesus; you did not drop a series of conclusions on us and demand our acceptance. You gave us a faith to be tested and tried. Before the certitude and the peace come the questioning and the struggle. We have to question before we can truly accept. I do not think you want people who will passively nod their heads like so many puppets to whatever you say. You want us to take the risk of exploring, trying, and seeking, with all the pain and purification that those involve.

I believe in order to understand. It is like looking at a stained glass window from the outside: the image is almost unintelligible. The same window, looked at from the inside, is radiant with meaning. My mind would never have led me to believe in the Trinity. But believing it as revealed, I can see that it points to a kind of community life in God, and that fits together coherently. Seen from within, it is congruent.

I find it encouraging, Jesus, that you expressed discouragement. You knew what it was like to experience the seeming pointlessness of what you were doing, the sense that people were slow to believe, resistant to anything that upset their fixed attitudes. You must have felt that it was like writing on water. That rings a bell. We are slow to accept change, even change for the better.

Faith and reason, heart and head – we need both. And it is prayer that brings them together. Then the tongue of the dumb can be loosed, the person can be lifted up and stand.

? *'What were you arguing about on the way?' (Mark 9:34)*

The apostles must have been embarrassed when you put this question to them; you had caught them out. They had been arguing about which of them was the greatest. 'I'm better than you.' 'No, you're not, I am.' Childish, isn't it? The stuff of kindergarten playgrounds, though found in all sorts of human structures, from academia to business to religion. 'I have the latest model car. It has ABS, SIPS, DVD player, aircon, GSM computer mapping, remote centralised locking, all as standard. Are you still driving last year's?' We measure our greatness by what we have, not even by what we are.

In the synagogue the rabbi sang, 'I am your lowly servant.' The first cantor sang, 'I am dust and ashes.' The second cantor sang, 'I am a nobody.' The secretary nudged his neighbour, pointed and said, 'Look who thinks he's a nobody.'

The greasy pole, the rat-race, who's in and who's out, who's up and who's down, who has the ear of the boss and who does not. Climb to the top by standing on the head of the other. Survival of the fittest. Election years are the year of the handshake, and so on and on.

But you say that authority is the power to serve, not to dominate. Power is a means to an end, not an end in itself, the end being the betterment of the person. Power is not meant to be self-serving and must operate within a moral framework.

Look at those old documentary films about the rise to power of Adolf Hitler. How the crowds worshipped him! How they shared by proxy in his gorging, gluttonous love of power! 'One people, one fatherland, one leader!' 'Sieg, Heil!' 'Heil, Hitler!' He appropriated religious language and symbols to his use, and people gave him a loyalty which should have been given to none but God. And, in the end, he returned their self-sacrifice and devotion by despising them, saying they were weak, not hard enough, not worthy of a leader like him.

You turn all those values upside down, Jesus, by pointing to a child as the example. A child has no illusions about itself; it is dependent, it knows it and is not ashamed to be. You said, 'Whoever wants to be first must be last of all and servant of all.' It is the givers rather than the takers who are remembered in the end.

? *'Salt is good; but if salt loses its saltiness, how can you season it?'*
(Mark 9:49)

Yes, Jesus, I know salt is good for seasoning food; just a little brings out the best in it. I know it is used in preserving food. I know it was used in the past to disinfect wounds, hurtful but helpful. It was also used as a salary, before money was widely circulated, given to those said to be worth their salt, a ready means of facilitating exchange among travellers.

I think what you are saying is that those who bring out the best in people, who preserve what is good, who help healing processes by preventing things from going sour or rotten, who facilitate exchange between people – those you count as among your followers.

I know people of all kinds, Jesus, who perform those and other similar functions. They are Christians, Muslims, Jews, atheists, agnostics, and those who could not put themselves in any category. Many of them do not count themselves as among your followers, and would be surprised that you considered them such. It reminds me of what your servant, Augustine of North Africa, said, 'There are many whom God has and the church does not have; and there are many whom the church has and God does not have.'

You always had a soft spot, Jesus, for those who were 'outsiders', for the rejects, those considered not good enough, who had not made the religious grade, the ones that the pious did not want to be seen with. You marvelled at the faith of a Roman centurion and commented that 'Many will come from east and west and will eat with Abraham and Isaac and Jacob in the kingdom of heaven.'

Those who saw themselves as the insiders you found pretty heavy weather; they caused you a lot of grief. In fact, they were the instruments of bringing about your death; you threatened their closed and precious arrangements. They were concerned with rules, you with attitudes. They made religion something that cramped and stifled people instead of an agency of human liberation. What you began in mysticism they ended in politics.

I know, too, that if salt becomes wet, there is no use in drying it; it has lost its saltiness and can not be re-seasoned. Once lost, it is gone. I think you are saying, Jesus, that no one has a guaranteed position as a follower of yours. Being a follower is not about position at all, in fact. It is about relationships. These are dynamic, like riding the waves of the sea, the source of salt, not static, like acquiring and holding an official position of Follower.

I notice, Jesus, that you answered your questioners with a question. They had asked you, 'Is it lawful for a man to divorce his wife?' In fact, divorce was universally accepted in the world of your day. Your question directed them back to the sources, ignoring what had developed between Moses' time and your own.

You opened up a new way of looking at the issue by saying that a man who divorces his wife and marries another commits adultery against her. Their view was that adultery could be committed only against a man. You rejected the double standard.

But you set a new and higher standard: you said that anyone who divorces and marries another is guilty of adultery. This was so radical that your followers questioned you about it afterwards to make sure they had not misunderstood you. They even said – with a touch of irony, I think – that, if that were the case, it would be better not to marry at all!

You knew you were setting a huge challenge before them, so you said, 'Not everyone can accept this teaching ... Let anyone accept this who can.' You knew human weakness, Jesus, but you still paid us the compliment of asking us to reach high.

You always asked for self-denial for the sake of the rule of your Father, didn't you? You wanted the world to be as God willed it. And for that, change was necessary at the level of personal relations. Change could not come without cost in personal effort and sacrifice, and you tried in every way to make that option clear. If we want to achieve what we have never achieved, we have to do what we have never done before.

What takes my breath away, Jesus, is this: you knew that what you were saying went utterly against the grain of the conventional wisdom of your time, but you still said it. And you said it as unconditionally as it is possible to say anything. You did not hesitate to brush aside centuries of tradition to the contrary. You asked people to reach up to high ideals; you did not lower the ideal to accommodate human weakness. Your desire to see your Father's will done was absolute. Only one thing counted: doing the will of God your Father.

? *'Why do you call me good?' (Mark 10:18)*

The man had addressed you as 'Good Teacher'. Was he trying to flatter you or was he genuine? I am not sure, Jesus, but I think he was genuine. You looked at him and loved him. You were nothing if not perceptive, and if he had been trying to butter you up, you would not have missed it. You knew what was in people. In that case, your response might have been short and sharp; you weren't one to fall for sweet talk.

Your answer to him was to pose the question, and then add, 'No one is good but God alone.' A strange reply, Jesus. Of course, God is the Good who makes good. I know that. Were you trying to re-direct him from yourself towards your Father? Did you want to focus his attention on the one and only who matters, to move him to re-assess priorities? All the time you were pointing beyond yourself to your Father. You said, 'I am the way.' Not the goal, but the way to it. Were you saying, in effect, 'Do not stop with me; go ahead and look further. I am the mediator with God, the one who shows you the way to him. Give him everything you have got; hold nothing back, and he will reward you'? Were you saying that God is a jealous God who looks for nothing less than all?

The man who approached you was excited and passionate. You put before him the challenge to renounce his many possessions in the service of the poor. You made it as attractive for him as you could; you promised him treasure in heaven if he would do it. But it was more than he was prepared to do. The treasure was the problem.

When it came to the moment of choice, he backed off. He did not make the commitment you sought. The cost of discipleship was one he was not prepared to pay. Is it harsh to think that he was enthusiastic but shallow?

I cannot condemn him, Jesus, because I see in him an image of myself, and that scares me. He refused your call. Was he the only person in the gospel to do so honestly and explicitly? With me, it is different. I have spoken a yes to you, but sometimes lived a no. A promise made and withdrawn is worse than a promise never given. Would you look at me and love me, as you did him?

? *'What is it you want me to do for you?' (Mark 10:36)*

Jesus, those two brothers, James and John, irritate me. They were so damned brazen. Imagine saying to you, or indeed anyone, 'We want you to do whatever we ask of you.' Who did they think you were? A puppet on their string? A magician with nothing to do but satisfy their whims? They got their pushiness from their mother; she was the pioneer of assertiveness training.

I do not know how you were patient with them, Jesus, but you were. Their request would have been understandable – perhaps – from a five-year-old, but from two grown men it was embarrassing.

You met their request with a question. How often you did that, Jesus! It was your wake-up call. You asked them if they were able to drink the cup that you must drink, or be baptised with the baptism that you would be baptised with. You asked them if they could share your destiny as the suffering servant of God. And what was their answer? 'We are able.' Just like that – no problem. Did they think of what they were saying, the bubble-heads? And where were they when the time came to fulfil their promise? – under the floor-boards!

This is one of the few questions, Jesus, that you asked twice. Just a little later you put it to a blind man. In reply he asked you for sight. And you answered him, 'Go; your faith has made you well.' Immediately he regained his sight and followed you on your way. His request was born of a pressing need which refused to be silenced. James and John's was the product of blind ambition. The sightless man saw the essentials while James and John set their eyes on trivia.

Jesus, I thank God for not always giving me what I asked for. Some of it was short-sighted, or even silly. You teach me to pray for what is real, you work with me in my deepest needs: 'Give us this day our daily bread.' My task is to know those needs and respond to them. Give me a sense of your priorities, your values. Help me to see with your eyes. Then I will want what you want for me, and you will give it to me, a divine conspiracy, the two of us breathing together.

?
• *'Are you able to drink the cup that I must drink, or be baptised with the baptism that I am baptised with?' (Mark 10:38)*

I go back, Jesus, to the question you put to James and John. You put it to me also. What is my answer?

I am glad you asked me, because it gives me the incentive to think about it. I take your question to mean, 'Do you know what you're doing? Do you know what you are letting yourself in for?' And, beyond that general question, I think it means, 'Can you enter into my emptying of self?'

Jesus, you constantly speak about renunciation of self. Anyone coming to you looking for a message of self-gratification would go away disappointed. I live in a culture which is deeply self-centred, which applauds the independent, self-assured person, the one who can achieve self-fulfilment alone, but which is at the same time a culture that longs for community.

There is something in me which wants community, but does not want to pay the price for it. The price is self-giving. That self-giving includes an active hope for what the other can become with the help of my solidarity. You call me to be a builder of community, that is, to be open and available to receive the gift of the other; to be able to help and to be helped, to be responsible for each other, to care.

I want freedom and then, in the next moment, like a child, expect God's intervention to save me from the consequences of my exercise of it. If God were to intervene in that way, what would be left for me to do? You never take from me the freedom to determine my attitudes.

I want certainty but do not want to be hemmed in or dictated to. You offer two basic certainties: the certainty of being infinitely loved, and the certainty of being capable of loving without limits.

There has to be a dying to self before there can be a growing to life. That is the simple but demanding message implied in your question. If I lose myself for others, then I find myself. And then a joyful community can begin to be born.

?• *'Is it not written, "My house shall be called a house of prayer for all the nations"?' (Mark 11:17)*

Jesus, I love that phrase – a house of prayer for all the nations. It is so all-embracing, so far and wide beyond the limitations of the local. The community of your followers is called to live, not for themselves alone, but for all the nations. It exists for that purpose.

I think I know why they killed you, Jesus: you gave a universal message to a people who could not see beyond the group, their group. They were narrow of mind, limited in imagination. They had 'their' God, 'their' teaching, 'their' temple. They thought of themselves as faithful to them, but in reality they co-opted them to their private agenda. They had slipped into the mind-set of 'God is on our side'. How many crimes have been committed in the name of that foolishness, Jesus, in the course of human history! How many cruelties, persecutions, wars even, have been fought with that rallying cry! Tsar Boris Godunov of Russia had it stamped on each of the nine thousand links that made up his chain-mail suit of armour. German soldiers in World War One had it embossed on the buckles on their belts: *Gott mit uns*. They forgot to ask whether they were on God's side, and to answer that question by reference to objective standards.

God is not the God of any party, group, or sect. The priest-politicians of your people, Jesus, were right in their calculating way to say that it was better for one man – you – to die for the sake of the people than for the whole nation to be destroyed. If your message caught the human imagination, then their local particularities, their hold on the copyright of God would be lost. They saw the implications of your message. The dividing walls would be broken down and the whole of humanity would enter the temple. All the nations would be God's chosen people. That would lead to their losing their reserved seats at the banqueting table in the kingdom of heaven. That was something they were not prepared to accept. For them, with their tunnel vision, another's gain meant their loss.

Deliver us, Jesus, from holy huddles; they are so self-approving, so narrow, so petty, so exclusive. They bind people in fear: 'We would lose our identity if we opened to all comers'. They fall into the great sin – idolatry. I do not mean the idolatry of elevating a creature to the status of creator, but that of reducing the creator to the status of creature.

God, you are one. You alone are God, you alone are sovereign. May you be praised forever in the whole world which is your house of prayer for all the nations.

? *'Did the baptism of John come from heaven, or was it of human origin?' (Mark 11:30)*

You had been challenged, Jesus, by the leaders of your people, the chief priests, the scribes and the elders, on a question dear to their hearts: 'By what authority are you doing these things?' Authority: not just any authority; what concerned them was their authority. They saw you – and they were right – as a threat to their view of their authority. For them, authority was self-justifying, not a means to an end, but an end in itself. You said that it must meet a moral purpose and be exercised morally in the service of the person.

In principle, of course, they agreed entirely, but the people were simple and unlettered and needed clear answers, so, in practice, things had to be different … We give people what they need, a firm hand, simple answers … for their own good, you understand.

This incident, Jesus, rings so true to life. People in authority are frightened; they feel their power – which they equate with authority – is called into question. They think in terms of official statements, precedents which may safely and legitimately be followed – subject to prior approval by the competent authority.

Why not just look at an issue on its merits? They were not able for that. For them that was unwise, imprudent, too risky, too large a jump for the mind trained in the ways of drawing conclusions from previously stated and approved principles.

When they challenged you, you threw a question back at them. You had a strong personality, Jesus, to be able to take on the high and mighty and disconcert them so. When you did it, they were unable to face your question honestly. They could not bring themselves to say that John's baptism was either from heaven or from earth. So they fudged, saying 'We do not know.' They had grown so used to politicising issues – Will it work? How will people react? How can it be reconciled with previous positions? – that they were not able to face them simply. They could not see that truth is its own authority. But you said, 'The truth shall make you free.' I love you for that, Jesus.

I have a confession to make, Jesus: with unashamed *schaden-freude*, I delight in seeing the devious upended by their devious-ness. It gives me voluptuous pleasure. I love to see you take the sup-posedly innocent question posed by the tricky and used it to dis-comfit them. I think it saddened you, though, Jesus, to see them so obdurate, so unwilling to let go of doctrinaire positions and face issues on their merits.

> **?** *'Have you not read this scripture: "The stone which the builders re-*
> **•** *jected has become the cornerstone; this was the Lord's doing, and it*
> *is amazing in our eyes"?' (Mark 12:10)*

Jesus, this reminds me of something that happened at the first Vatican Council of the Catholic Church in 1869. A group of missionary bishops from Africa asked the Pope of the day to lift the curse of Cain from Africa. They saw the continent as a place of witchcraft, slavery, polygamy, inter-tribal warfare, infanticide, and many other evils. They were right; it was all of those. The bishops saw this as evidence of God's curse on Africans as the descendants of Cain, the murderer of his brother, Abel. In that they were wrong, and I am glad the Pope did not go along with them.

Europe of the day saw itself as the bearer of Christianity, civilisation and commerce to Africa, 'the dark continent'. Europeans assumed their superiority to Africans; it was not a point they argued but a supposition they took for granted. But the most conservative estimates of indigenous people killed in the process of European colonial expansion is fifty million – in the name of civilisation

Today, Europe has largely abandoned the Christian faith. There are many reasons for this, but it has not been without arrogance, seeing itself as breaking free from outmoded restraints, and even from God as from an unnecessary hypothesis. And Europe is dying, though it is asleep to the fact. It has lost shared values, and with it a sense of community. The individual is everything and selfishness is widespread. Europe has lost respect for human life, and its population is ageing and declining. With the loss of faith, the heart has gone out of Europe, and it is looking for substitutes in possessions, pleasure and power.

Africa today still has the same problems as before, perhaps to a greater degree, and some new ones as well, like AIDS. Yet, despite everything, Africa still has a warm heart, a deep humanity, an orientation to life and a capacity for love. I believe, Jesus, this is because Africa, unlike Europe, has not abandoned faith in God. Whether Africans are Christian, Moslem, or followers of traditional religion, they believe in God. For them, God is not a point to be argued but a self-evident reality.

Faith in God is the stone which Europeans have rejected. It is the cornerstone of Africa and much of the Third World. This was the Lord's doing, and it is amazing in our eyes. Maybe we in the First World will hear the judgment that 'the kingdom of God is taken away from you and given to a people that produces the fruits of the kingdom'.

? *'Why are you putting me to the test? Whose head is this, and whose title?' (Mark 12:15-16)*

When the Pharisees and Herodians heard your question, Jesus, I wonder if its words resonated with them. Did they recall the prohibition in the law of Moses, 'Do not put the Lord your God to the test'? Of course, they did not – could not – have recognised you as God made man; I do not expect that, but is it not surprising that they did not pause for a moment for second thoughts, knowing they were being disingenuous?

Their question was posed to trip you up: 'Is it lawful to pay taxes to the emperor, or not?' If you answered 'no', they would report you to the Roman administration which levied it. If you said 'yes', they would publicise your reply among the people, who resented the tax. Either way you would be caught.

You threw the matter back to them by asking to be shown the coin of payment, thereby underlining the fact that they paid the tax anyway. Then you asked your question, and they answered, 'The emperor's.' You said to them, 'Give to the emperor the things that are the emperor's, and to God the things that are God's.' Being amazed by your answer, they became silent, they left you and went away.

Brilliantly done, Jesus, a magnificent retort! You took them on at their own game and beat them. You met them on their own terms and shut them up. And yet, Jesus – forgive me for saying this – I cannot help feeling that your answer was clever more than it was wise. After all, the things of the emperor are also the things of God, are they not? Is not life in all its aspects under God's rule? It sounds as if you implied that the things of the emperor were outside God's dominion – and that cannot be right. Was your reply not just a little too clever? Or am I reading too much into it?

But I should try to answer your question as if posed to me. Whose image is on me? God's is; I have been made in his image. Whose name is on me? The one you gave me when I was baptised, when you called me and made me yours. I did nothing to deserve it, it is purely a gift, but your imprint, your stamp, your seal is on me. Why did you call me rather than another? I do not know. I can think of many people who would give you a better return for your gift than I do, yet the fact is that you chose me.

And I have another name, the name of Christian. I hope that in me it is more than an honorary title with nominal or passive commitment. If I ever found myself put to the test, brought before a court and charged with being a Christian, I hope there would be enough evidence for a conviction.

? *'Is not this the reason you are wrong, that you know neither the* **•** *scriptures nor the power of God?' (Mark 12:24)*

Jesus, you know how to throw a heavy punch. But I think I understand the reason why. The Sadducees, to whom you first posed the question, had been not a little flippant towards the scriptures and the power of God. They presented a far-fetched story about a woman who had married seven brothers, one after the other as the previous one died. They then posed the question, 'In the resurrection, whose wife will she be?' It was a purpose-built argument, designed to reduce the resurrection to absurdity. It also assumed that life after the resurrection is substantially the same as before. But our yesterday, today and tomorrow are one single instant in the eyes of your Father.

You did not compromise with those who were disingenuous on questions of truth, who wanted to score a point or win an argument, even if it meant losing the truth. You brought their dishonesty out into the open and held it up to them: 'You are quite wrong.' After that, they no longer dared to ask you another question.

In a different way, this reminds me, Jesus, of a biblical scholar, one of the best of our time, who said that a person will learn more about the bible from trying to live it than from studying it. He could not be accused of being anti-intellectual as he had spent all his adult life in biblical scholarship. His point was about priorities. People who try to live the bible develop an affinity for it, they intuitively come to operate on its wavelength, their knowledge of it is experiential more than bookish.

The scriptures are full of paradoxes, symbols and enigmas – just as life itself is. The rational is too narrow, almost mechanistic in its limitations. You said, 'Whoever is not with me is against me, and whoever does not gather with me scatters.' But you also said, 'Whoever is not against you is for you.' Your follower, Paul, wrote, 'Bear one another's burdens, and in this way you will fulfil the law of Christ.' Only four verses later he wrote, 'All must carry their own burdens.' Logicians would tear their hair out in frustration at such lack of logic. But the statements are not irrational; they go beyond reason. I think that was why you taught in parables. Parables urge us to look beyond the immediate to a deeper level of meaning, to look not so much *at* a story as *through* it, to see what it points to beyond itself. How foolish it would be to imagine that a person could ever encompass any of your mysteries in an intellectual system! Only God can understand God. And the best way to begin to know God is to love people.

? '*How can the scribes say that the Messiah is the Son of David?*
• *David himself calls him Lord; so how can he be his son?*' (Mark
12:35, 37)

In this situation, Jesus, you raised an issue yourself. You used your question to draw your hearers into reflecting on the Messiah, the anointed one of God, his messenger to his chosen people. According to popular belief, he had to be a descendant of King David. You asked how it was that, since David called the Messiah Lord, the Messiah would also be his son or descendant. A father would not call his son Lord.

Jesus, I think you were trying to open people's minds beyond their narrow boundaries. You recognised that, although you were indeed descended from David, that was not important. What counted was that you inherited his spiritual mantle, without the political associations then current. You did not want a messiahship that was a campaign for political independence.

The gospel says that your hearers, a large crowd, listened to you with delight. Why, I wonder? Was it that you had just silenced the Sadducees to the delight of the scribes; but now it was the scribes' turn to be silenced. Were you poking fun at them? Were you using gentle irony and ridicule to reduce someone's narrow preconceptions to absurdity? Perhaps. A Jewish acquaintance of mine once told me he could tell from reading the gospel that you were a Jew just by your sense of humour.

You spoke of people hiring trumpeters to advertise their charity; picking from the eye of another the speck of sawdust they can see through the plank in their own eye; guests of honour deliberately sitting far from the top table in order to attract attention when they are moved up; those who strain out a gnat while swallowing a camel, or who put a lamp under a bed instead of on a table; the oppressive rulers who demanded to be called benefactors. You asked whether grapes grow on a cactus or figs on a thistle; you mocked the 'blind guides'; you invited fishermen to be fishers of men; you asked your hearers what they were out into the desert to see – was it a reed shaken in the wind or a man wearing fine clothes? Two of your followers, tied to their mother's apron strings, who then got above themselves, you nicknamed 'sons of thunder'. And I imagine you smiled, perhaps chuckled, when the Canaanite woman outwitted you with her lively repartee.

Humour is a safety-valve, Jesus. It dissolves tension and helps free us of stubbornness. We learn and appreciate more easily what we laugh at.

? *'Do you see these great buildings? Not one stone will be left here upon another; all will be thrown down.' (Mark 13:2)*

The people of your time, Jesus, were impressed by the temple in Jerusalem that you spoke of. Even today we are awed by the massive blocks of stone that form its Western wall, and all the more so as they were put in place before the age of machinery, when human muscle power was the only engine. From start to finish, the temple had taken eighty-three years to build, and it was completed only six years before the Romans destroyed it. Today, Jews and Moslems fight each other about its remains. Some want to rebuild it, to reconstruct the past, to go back to 'the good old days'. Others claim it as theirs and are prepared to kill for it.

Yes, Jesus, we are impressed by great buildings. That was the reason for their construction in the first place – they were built to impress. The cathedrals of Europe built in the Middle Ages could be seen a long way off; they were the tallest buildings of their time, and they made a statement – we have power, we are the biggest, and we are here to stay. The same was true of factory chimneys in the nineteenth century; they impressed and they intimidated. They made the individual feel small. But many of them have already crumbled to dust, replaced by the new towers of financial institutions. They, too, will pass and be replaced. Human institutions peak only to collapse. History books are full of the stories of the rise and fall of empires.

You had already told your people that you had not chosen the nation for the sake of the holy place, but the holy place for the sake of the nation. In your estimation people came first, then institutions, even 'holy' ones, such as the temple. Institutions are a means to an end, which is the service of the person. We keep messing up your priorities, don't we, Jesus? We build up institutions, succumbing to the subtle seduction of power, until they both subsume the individual and pervert the purpose for which they were founded. Armies established for defence become instruments of oppression to their own people.

We are in a special class of slow learners. The old must give way to the new, it must die so that the new may be born. Help me to learn the lessons of the past, Jesus, not to repeat its mistakes.

43

? *'Let her alone. Why do you trouble her?'* (Mark 14:6)

The woman you spoke of had performed an act of exuberant generosity, pouring expensive ointment over your head. She was not counting the cost, or saving some for later – she even broke the jar. The ointment was all gone in one enthusiastic burst of extravagance. What she did was foreign to the parsimonious, penny-pinching side of us. Her wastefulness was like your own, Jesus, creating flowers where no one sees them, causing rain to fall on the sea, creating tiny insects no one has ever heard of, putting many seeds in the heart of a tomato when just one alone would be sufficient for a new plant to germinate. That is your way. Love diffuses itself.

People objected to the waste, and they voiced it in the name of the poor. But the poor are with them and with me always, and I pass them by where they sleep in the doorways of shops and the corners of railway stations. I identify sufficiently with the poor to complain on their behalf but not enough to share what I have with them. I blame someone else and do nothing.

You defended the woman, when it would have been easier to go with the flow and join in criticising her as improvident. It was your way to defend the defenceless. Jesus, sometimes I am strong with the weak and weak with the strong. It is a trait I do not like. Give me the courage to stand up, and stand alone, if that is what is needed, and especially to stand up for those who have no one to stand up for them.

Women are often bullied by men, Jesus, aren't they? It is a nasty side to our character. You challenged prevailing attitudes to women: you talked with the Samaritan woman at the well, a big taboo in those days; you ignored the rules about ritual impurity when touched by a woman with a haemorrhage; you allowed the sinful woman to approach you in the house of Simon the Pharisee; you were gentle towards the woman caught in adultery when men, exulting in their sense of power, were prepared to stone her.

Those actions of yours went against the grain, Jesus, and they faulted you for them. You taught a new attitude by what you did. You said of the woman who anointed your body, 'Wherever the good news is proclaimed in the whole world, what she has done will be told in remembrance of her.' Was she perhaps the first to recognise you as the Christ, the anointed one?

? *'Are you asleep? Could you not keep awake one hour? Are you still*
• *sleeping and taking your rest?' (Mark 14:37, 41)*

Jesus, it was after your last supper with your followers, and you suffered in anticipation of the death you knew was coming. You looked for a gesture of human solidarity, for some human comfort, a little warmth – and there was none. Your followers were asleep.

There is more than one way of being asleep: 'I did not see, I did not hear, I did not know, I did not think …' 'I did not see the documentary about famine in Africa. I did not hear about the suicide of the drug addict. I did not know my child was lonely and could talk to no one. I did not think I had drunk over the limit …' Sometimes, Jesus, I close my eyes, my ears, my mind so that I will not see, hear, know or think. And I tell myself I am without blame. I say, 'If only I had seen, heard, known …'

Wake me up, Lord. You gave me eyes to see and ears to hear. You gave me a mind to think with. You gave me a memory to learn from the past. You gave me an imagination to dream for the future. You gave me a heart to care. You gave me a will to decide. You ask me to use these gifts you gave me. That is not asking too much.

My neighbour is in need. Who is my neighbour? All humanity. No, more than that – all creation. Help me to grow beyond the level of the infant who can look at mother or father blankly, without recognition. Do not allow me to sit for ever on the fence of indecision, of non-commitment, waiting for some perfect moment when all will be clear and a decision will be easy. Let me live in the here and now, doing what I can in this time, this place, this bundle of circumstances, with this messed-up person that I am.

You spoke of 'one hour'. Help me to recognise the uniqueness of the present moment; it is unrepeatable. You do not ask for a year, or even a day. Each moment is a unique gift from you, with its own message of the infinite. Can I be with you for just one hour, can I be awake for even that length of time, to be aware of myself, to know what is happening to me, to be alive in this world, to wake up? When I am awake to myself then I will be awake to you also. I will know your presence when I am present to myself.

Jesus, you do not ask me to be successful; you do ask me to be faithful. And you have a right to ask it. I will do what I can; may you do what you will.

? *'Have you come out with swords and clubs to arrest me as though I were a bandit?' (Mark 14:48)*

There is more than a little, Jesus, of the bully's bravery about this posse of Judas and his henchmen coming to arrest you, armed with swords and clubs. You had been with them day after day in the temple and they had not laid hands on you. They found their courage in the dark, in a night ambush by mob. This was their hour and the power of darkness, so that the scriptures might be fulfilled. It does not make for pleasant reading, this sordid account of bogus courage, reliant on the force of arms.

It reminds me of the incident, not long before, where some men had complained about the woman wasting the ointment on you. It was Judas who was in action there also, voicing that complaint, not because he cared about the poor, but because he was a thief; he kept the common purse and used to steal what was put into it. His cowardly criticism of the woman rings true to character.

Peter was so different – impetuous, generous, foolish Peter. He came to your defence in his own unthinking way. He took out his sword and cut off the ear of Malchus, the servant of the high priest. That, too, was true to form: he liked the ways of power; it was he who had reacted at the thought that you would suffer and be crucified, he who had rashly promised that, even if everyone else deserted you, he would lay down his life for you. You knew him better than he knew himself.

You responded to Peter's action by saying, 'No more of this!' and you touched the servant's ear and healed him, adding, 'Put your sword back into its place, for all who take the sword will perish by the sword. Am I not to drink the cup that the Father has given me?' Those words – 'all who take the sword will perish by the sword' – how true they are! There have been 240 wars since 1945. In the nineteen nineties, over 170 million people lost their rights and property in war, while 2 million children were killed.

And what of the other disciples? They deserted you and fled: collegiality in action! Jesus, save me from big talk and big promises. What I have seen in life is that the people of big talk and promises are the ones who fail when the time of testing comes; they relied on themselves. It is the small, the weak, the poor, the despised, the nobodies who are strong in that moment. Although they also are afraid, they have learned to rely on you, and that is what makes them strong. Jesus, you gave me two eyes, two ears and only one mouth; may I learn from that.

? *'My God, my God, why have you forsaken me?'* (Mark 15:34)

This, your most searching question, Jesus, is the only one in the gospel you addressed, not to a human being, but to God. It was a follow-up to the one prayer of petition in the gospel which received the answer 'no', the prayer you offered in the garden of Gethsemane: 'Father, for you all things are possible; remove this cup from me; yet, not what I want, but what you want.' In the dark and difficult moments of my life I stand beside you and ask the same question.

This question leads me into the mystery of suffering, your suffering, Jesus, and mine. A mystery is not so much something I can never understand as something about which I can never understand enough. The word 'mystery' is not a *No Entry* sign forbidding me to go further. A mystery is not a problem to be solved but a paradox to be lived. Suffering can be a school of solidarity with you and with all those around the world who have ever suffered. May I not seek to abscond from it.

When I find myself in suffering, Lord, none of this means anything. All I can do is voice my pain, 'My God, I call by day and you give no reply; I call by night and I find no peace. Do not leave me alone in my distress; come close, there is none else to help.' I am like an addict experiencing cold turkey, 'Parched as burnt clay is my throat, my tongue cleaves to my jaws. People stare at me and gloat. Lord, do not leave me alone.' There must be few forms of suffering harder to bear than a sense of being abandoned, that no one is listening and no one cares because they are absorbed in themselves. This was truly your dark night of the soul. What a difference it would have made to you if even one of your disciples had stayed awake for just a few hours!

Often, Lord, your absence seems more real than your presence. Prayer seems like talking to myself, and expecting an answer mere foolishness. Your servant, Job, voiced it on my behalf: 'A man becomes a laughing-stock to his friends, if he cries to God and expects an answer.' Why do you not answer, Lord? Are you silent, or am I deaf? I will live with this uncertainty. Better that than a facile solution which solves nothing, an explanation which explains by explaining away. Jesus, let me just hold on. I know that the main problem in my prayer is not 'the absence of God' but 'the absence of me'. Prayer is believing that I live in the mystery of God.

? *'If you love those who love you, what reward do you have? Do not even the tax collectors do the same? And if you greet only your brothers and sisters, what more are you doing than others? Do not even the Gentiles do the same?' (Matthew 5:46-47)*

You set high standards, Jesus – sometimes, it seems, impossibly high. Many of the great thinkers of the world said, 'Don't do to others what you would not like them to do to you.' That's easy to understand, even if demanding to live.

But you went further. You put the challenge positively: 'Do to others as you would have them do to you.' That goes a lot further, does it not, Jesus? Do you really think I can measure up to such a standard? You tell me to love my neighbours, and also to love my enemies – they are often the same people. This business of loving my neighbour: it's a beautiful ideal, but some neighbours are not lovable, are they? You are saying that whether I like them or not, indeed, even if I hate them, I should reach beyond the dislikes and differences. I should still do what is for their good, respect them, care for them and actively seek out ways of building them up. That is very hard, Jesus. Did you know what you were asking?

But you were not content even with that. You went still further, saying, 'Just as I have loved you, you also should love one another.' How did you love us? To the extent of dying for us, even though we were guilty and you were innocent. That is what you are asking of us. Are you serious, Jesus? Do you not understand how risky that is, how vulnerable it would make me? With such unconditional love, I would be lied to, exploited, manipulated, torn apart and devoured.

That frightens me so much I would almost consider settling for what common sense dictates – half-loving and half-living, half-hoping and half-caring. But that is a slow, suffocating death. I know it is in discovering others that I come to discover myself; I know it is in loving others that I come to love myself and love you, but it is so damned hard. Can you not make it easier, Jesus?

In the evening of life, I will be judged on love. To love is to be vulnerable. If I love anybody or anything, I may end with my heart being broken. Apart from heaven, the only place where I am free of the risks that loving entails is hell. And hell is being unable to love, carefully looking after myself. The only way for a follower of yours to live is to risk love. As long as I love another person less than I love myself, I will not really succeed in loving myself. But if I love all people, including myself, I will love them as one person. That is the measure of my love of God. Love is indivisible.

? *'Is not life more than food and the body more than clothing? Look at*
• *the birds of the air; they neither sew nor reap nor gather into barns,*
and yet your heavenly Father feeds them. Are you not of more value
than they? And can any of you by worrying add a single hour to
your span of life?' (Matthew 6:25-27)

I think I hear what you say, Jesus, but were you not exaggerating, carried away with rhetorical flourishes? You want me, I know, to be single-minded, focused on the Reign of God, concerned above all else with trying to make my bit of the world – especially myself – into the kind of place your Father wants it to be.

You are not issuing an invitation to laziness. I have never seen a lazy bird, and neither have you, I am sure. You are not saying that I should sit back and do nothing, waiting for food to fall into my mouth or clothes to appear on my back. Is it that you do not want me to be possessed by possessions or, even worse, possessed by possessiveness? That is an anxious state of mind forever driven by the desire for more, pursuing an incessant 'progress' that never ends in contentment, but condemns all of us to emptiness of soul.

I remember Imelda Marcos of the Philippines with the – was it four? – thousand pairs of shoes. I remember Mobutu of Zaïre who had constructed an international airport near his home village so he could drop in to see his mother occasionally, and the Russian empress with the eleven thousand dresses, and Ivan the Terrible, also of Russia, his throne studded with nine thousand diamonds. Greed never says, 'I have enough'; it always wants more, its infantile maw reaching out to grab. Your heavenly Father has given enough to meet everyone's need, not enough for everyone's greed.

I feel almost virtuous alongside them, Jesus. I know I will never equal their greed. But that is lack of opportunity, not choice: a poor person can be possessive of a jam-jar.

The spirit of 'I want' is strong in me. I am possessive of my time and energy, even though I know that possessiveness divides while sharing unites. I have my ideas, my agenda, my ambitions, and I can be single-minded in their pursuit. You are asking me to let them go, taking on instead your Father's ideas, agenda and ambitions with the same single-mindedness. You want us to live life in communion, in solidarity, not as atomised individuals.

And I notice, Jesus, you used the word 'worry' twice. The possessive person worries about the possibility of loss, theft, damage. There is freedom in being ready to share, being willing to live for the other more than the self. Help me to let go and to let God ... Then I will know freedom.

? *'Why do you see the speck in your neighbour's eye, but do not notice*
• *the log in your own eye? Or how can you say to your neighbour,*
'Let me take the speck out of your eye,' while the log is in your own
eye?' (Matthew 7:3-4)

I know, Jesus, that the faults I criticise most severely in others are those I refuse to acknowledge in myself. I do not often realise how much I reveal about myself when I launch into an earnest and high-minded denunciation of another; I betray the yawning gap in myself. Suspicion haunts the guilty mind.

I can be aggressively busy in examining other people's consciences for them. Maybe it is an occupational hazard. But I should direct those energies towards sorting myself out. It is the one part of the world I can do something about.

You are happy for me to judge actions, Jesus. How else could I learn the difference between right and wrong? But you draw the line before judging attitudes. It is difficult enough for me truly to understand my own attitudes, never mind anyone else's. And it is even worse if I go beyond that, and indulge in condemnation. Judgment belongs to God alone. Forgive me, Jesus.

If I did take the speck from my own eye, then I would see more clearly and be able to take the log from the other's. If I face the struggle, look my own demons in the eye, recognise them for what they are, call them by name and challenge them, then I will appreciate the effort involved in the struggle against evil.

Some of the most understanding and sympathetic people I have met with have been alcoholics and prostitutes. They are compassionate, suffering with sinners in the misery of their sins. They have a humanity, a warmth, about them that is so refreshing a change from the cold, dry seriousness of the righteous. Was that why you had a soft spot for them? A person could turn to them in trouble. All you would get from the righteous would be a scolding, or a lecture about pulling yourself together and snapping out of it.

One of your followers said that a spoonful of honey is better than a barrelful of vinegar. The critical one looks at the sin, demands an explanation, and asks 'Why?' The compassionate one looks at the sinner, thinks of what he or she could be, and asks 'Why not?' One looks at the past with a verdict, the other to the future with hope. How beautiful on the mountains are the feet of those who bring peace!

? *'Is there anyone among you who, if your child asks for bread, will give a stone? Or if the child asks for a fish, will give him a snake?'* *(Matthew 7:9-10)*

I like the pawpaw fruit, Jesus. It is juicy, sweet, and very refreshing on a hot day. It is easy to prepare for eating. You just take a knife, even a butter knife, and slice its soft flesh. A few drops of lemon juice give it an extra flavour. In the centre of the fruit are the seeds, hundreds of them, each about one third the size of a pea. If you take those seeds, rinse, dry and plant them, they become the next generation of pawpaw trees. Each of the several hundred seeds of one fruit has the potential to become a tree which, in its lifetime, will produce hundreds of fruits, each containing hundreds of seeds – and so on from generation to generation.

How many krill are there under the Antarctic ice-pack? Billions. Flowers grow on rubbish dumps, and grass in the corners of scrapyards. Young trees vandalised, hacked, carved, even burned, with torn branches stripping away some bark, still struggle for life, send out new shoots, never giving up, always forgiving, nurturing hope.

The birth of every child is a sign of fresh hope for humanity, a sign that God has not given up on us. And every one of the six thousand and more million people in the world is different, while sharing a common humanity. Diversity and unity. And every one is more than a mouth to be fed; it has head, heart and hands; it is a gift to be welcomed, not a danger to be feared.

I must return to your question, Jesus. No parent would give a hungry child a stone instead of bread, or a snake instead of a fish. I could not imagine it. The love of parents for children is one of the constants in a changing and sometimes evil world. Thank God for that.

But you were making a different point, that if no parent would refuse a child's request for food, then even less would our Father in heaven refuse our daily bread to us, his children. Hunger, poverty and disease come, not from God's will – that excuse is blasphemous – but from our injustice to our fellow humans, our unwillingness to share.

Jesus, you were God's first Word; creation was his second. You both are God's self-expression, his embodiment. You both say that God is forgiving and also for giving. Praise you.

? *'Are grapes gathered from thorns, or figs from thistles?' (Matthew 7:16)*

A rhetorical question, Jesus, one of many you asked to produce an effect. What effect? That I should open my eyes and look at what is going on. Every tree, every person, bears the fruit appropriate to itself.

You were talking, Jesus, about false prophets. You said they come in sheep's clothing but inwardly are ravenous wolves. What are the signs that might indicate who they are? One is that they feel certain about their answers.

A man who was impressed by the teaching of Siddartha Gautama once asked him, 'Are you a god or a magician?' He answered, 'I am neither a god nor a magician. I am one who is awake,' or, as we now say, the Enlightened One, the Buddha.

And then there was Socrates. He kept asking his students questions to get them to think so as to find answers for themselves – the Socratic method of education. Your Father is Socratic; he asked Job questions in order to bring him to self-understanding.

But there were others who were certain they had answers to questions. They had few doubts, lots of certainties. Stalin felt he had the answer to the problems of farming in the Soviet Union – collectivisation. He deliberately created a famine in the Ukraine in the late 1930s which killed six million small farmers, thereby removing opposition to his plans.

Another one who was sure of his answers was Adolf Hitler. He had the Final Solution to the Jewish Question – kill them. His determination to impose his will on Europe cost about fifty million people their lives, including some seven million Germans between 1939 and 1947, and no one knows how many more in the Cold War which resulted. In the Third World, the Cold War was hot, the superpowers fighting out their rivalries in wars of proxy.

Yet another was Mao Zedong of China. One of his successors, Deng Hsiao Ping, said that Mao was responsible for the deaths of about thirty million Chinese, especially through his industrialisation policy, the Great Leap Forward.

One feature of these men of definite answers is that they thought of people in the mass. Those who asked questions thought of people as individuals. Ideologies, those half-truths pretending to be whole truths, are teachings that bewitch. They put the mind on hold with set, prepared answers, where paradox, ambiguity and parable bring us nearer to the whole truth.

? *'Why do you think evil in your hearts?'* *(Matthew 9:4)*

Your have put your finger on it, Jesus. Evil begins in the heart, not outside of it, not in circumstances, environment, background or opportunity. The dividing line between good and evil runs through every human heart. There is in us – in me – an inclination to evil. I am fallen. The good I know I should do, I do not do, and the evil I know I should not do, I do. Evil has a fascination which calls out to me and I answer it. Evil is a mystery – why is it that I act against my good? Evil is like a shadow, the absence of light. Good comes from you as from an all-embracing source, and evil from many partial deficiencies.

What is the secret of evil? It points to the Ego in me. It says, 'Be your own man, do your own thing, why be dictated to by another? Life is short, make the most of it, look after yourself – no one else will. The important thing is to be happy. Hoist the flag of independence.'

But I am not independent, I cannot be. To imagine that I am is a dangerous myth. I am dependent. I did not call myself to birth, nourish, clothe or educate myself. I need others at every stage of my life. I do not stand alone. I need others and I owe them.

And I need you. Without you there is no ultimate meaning. To set myself apart from you, to shout in defiance, 'I will not serve', is to cut myself off from you who are the source of life.

And evil is self-destructive: it so exalts the self that it will cheerfully destroy anything to further its status, even to the extent of destroying itself. Evil is a lie. Coming from the father of lies, it is a false promise, a glittering jewel that turns out to be a bauble.

Whatever I do, or leave undone, promotes or prevents evil. It is in my hands. I have the free will that you gave me, the power of choice, the capacity to say yes or no to God and to good.

May I face the evil which is in me, acknowledge it in truth and call it by name. May I never try to sweep it under the carpet, or condone it through a parody of forgiveness. I know that you can bring good out of evil; may I never make that an excuse for not fighting evil in myself. When I pray, 'Deliver us from evil' may I mean it, and fight evil, starting with myself.

? *'Do you believe that I am able to do this?' (Matthew 9:28)*

You were followed from Jericho by a large crowd, Jesus, and there were two blind men sitting by the roadside. When they heard you were passing, they shouted, 'Lord, have mercy on us'. The crowd sternly ordered them to be quiet, but they shouted even more loudly, 'Have mercy on us, Lord.' They followed you into the house and went to you. They saw an opportunity and were not going to lose it. They were not going to be diverted from their purpose by the crowd. No embarrassment about drawing attention to themselves held them back. They were blind to the looks of annoyance on the faces of people who felt perhaps that the special occasion of your visit was being marred by this unseemly shouting.

These were blind men who actually wanted to see. There are other blind who do not: they prefer the dark, prefer not to see, hear or know, so as not to have to make a choice or commitment. They sit on the fence, living in the land of perpetual postponement, never doing today what they can put off till tomorrow. They go half-living through life, as if it were a dress rehearsal, not the real thing. You were close to people who were real, to those who knew what they wanted, who had a sense of reality and of priorities, people who focused on things that mattered, like sight if they were blind.

You put your question to them, Jesus, and they answered without hesitation, 'Yes, Lord.' What made them so sure? Had they heard about you from others or were they just putting on a brave face? I think it was the first, because when you touched them, saying, 'According to your faith let it be done to you,' their eyes were opened.

That phrase, 'according to your faith' was the heart of the matter. So many times you spoke of faith, and you did no healing without it. In your home village of Nazareth you were amazed at their unbelief and you could do no deed of power there.

You sought also to avoid sensationalism, Jesus, telling the men to remain silent. Your deeds of power were not magic; they were not done without us. You invite us to walk, you do not drag us. We are not meant to be passive spectators but active participants in the drama of life. And the healing was a sign that pointed beyond itself: from being outcasts, on the fringes of the town, the men resumed their place in the community.

What about me, Jesus? Do I believe that you are able to give me sight? Yes, Jesus, you have already done so. You open my eyes, you widen my horizons, you give me a mind to think with, a memory to learn from, and an imagination to dream with. Thank you.

? *'Are not two sparrows sold for a penny?' (Matthew 10:29)*

I know what you were getting at with the question, Jesus. It was a favourite theme of yours – that we should not be afraid, because we have one who protects us, God our Father. But sometimes I see only what is directly in front of me, not the wider picture. Sometimes I forget what I have learned from the past and so I am anxious about the future. A parishioner once said to me, 'Yesterday is history; tomorrow is a mystery; today is a gift – and that's why we call it the present.' How true! It is in the present that we experience the Presence.

You want us to let go of fear. Fear comes from our not understanding ourselves; it distorts self-knowledge. It causes, expresses and reinforces low self-esteem, even self-loathing. Fear is the great obstacle between us and reality. It corrupts. Because of it, we live below our best, turn inwards on ourselves, protecting ourselves. Fear is a barometer of self-love, and servile fear is the greatest enemy of love. But if we face the fears within, those without will have few terrors for us.

You are saying to us that we are not insignificant; we matter in God's eyes. For the most part, we are better than we think we are. I should never be afraid to accept the truth about myself – no matter how good it may be. You lift us up and give us hope. Nothing can release us from our fears as fully as an awareness of the unconditional love that God revealed to us in you.

The reason you give for not being afraid is that God is our Creator, and cares for us. Not even a sparrow falls to the ground without God's knowing it, and we are worth more than hundreds of sparrows. We count in the sight of God. Whatever our situation, whether we live or die, we are in the hands of God. God loves us, not because we were good and deserved it, because he is good and decided it. I might run from my fears but I would run to you as a brother.

What can I say in answer to your question, Jesus? Only one thing: Thank you. Thank you for saying, 'Fear not, I have overcome the world.'

? 'What did you go out into the wilderness to look at? A reed shaken
• by the wind? What then did you go out to see? Someone dressed in
soft robes? Look, those who wear soft robes are in royal palaces.
What then did you go out to see? A prophet?' (Matthew 11:7-9)

You spoke, Jesus, of John, your cousin, the last and greatest of the
Old Testament prophets, the one who brought that prophetic line to
fulfilment, who handed it over to you when he baptised you. He an-
nounced the coming of your rule. He called people to repentance,
especially by giving up cheating and oppression, and by giving to
the poor. John was a prophet, one whose task was to forth-tell the
present more than to foretell the future.

John was a rough diamond. He lived in the wilderness of Judea,
wore clothing of camel's hair with a leather belt around his waist,
and his food was locusts and wild honey. He was an unusual com-
bination, austere, even severe, but popular. Political correctness
was foreign to him. He was a man wholly dedicated to the truth,
publicly criticising Herod Antipas for his adulterous and incestu-
ous relationship with Herodias, wife of his brother Philip. He said
to him, 'It is not lawful for you to have your brother's wife.' That
was to cost him his head.

Jesus, when you spoke, you knew that John was not in the king's
palace but in his prison. He had sent his messengers to you, asking,
'Are you the one who is to come, or are we to wait for another?' He
was uncertain. You answered him in terms that he would have well
understood. You quoted the prophet Isaiah, 'Tell John what you
hear and see: the blind receive their sight, the lame walk, the lepers
are cleansed, the deaf hear, the dead are raised, and the poor have
good news brought to them.' You added what must have been a
personal message for him, 'Blessed is anyone who takes no offence
at me.'

I take comfort from the fact that John had doubts. People of
rock-like certainty scare me: they seem to have nothing to learn. Is
there a basic division, Jesus, in the world, between those who are
willing and able to learn, and those who are not?

I take comfort too, from your statement that the fulfilment of
human needs is a sign that the kingdom of God is present. That
gives hope to the many people of good will, not necessarily believ-
ers, who work for human betterment. I think God will more readily
forgive our sins against him, whom we cannot see, than against our
fellow humans, whom we can see. You give those people hope
when you said, 'Among those born of women, no one is greater
than John; yet the least in the kingdom of God is greater than he.'

? *'And you, Capernaum, will you be exalted to heaven?' (Matthew 11:23)*

Jesus, you made Capernaum your own town, and it was the centre of your activity in Galilee. It was there you began your ministry by teaching in the synagogue on the sabbath and driving a demon out of a man. There you healed the centurion's servant, the man with the palsy and Simon Peter's mother-in-law, and taught your disciples about greatness being measured in service. You did so many wonders there that the people of Nazareth, the village of your childhood, seem to have become jealous.

There is something strangely and sadly true to human nature that it was in the towns where you gave the most – Chorazin, Bethsaida and Capernaum – that you received the least. Why is that so? The most loved child is often the least grateful. The people most favoured become arrogant, take their position for granted, and demand still more. Like a leaf withering in the autumn, they curl around themselves, hollow inside.

You answered your own question, Jesus, saying, 'No, you will be brought down to Hades.' Hades was the 'non-world', the abode of the dead. Was it that, having lived for themselves alone, they got what they had chosen – themselves – were left to themselves, and died by themselves, the return of self-centredness? Was it the pride, or hubris, of 'We have nothing to learn from anyone'? Could it have been, 'We have Jesus among us, so we have no need to do anything; he will look after us'? Was it that they could not be bothered to listen, they had other interests to follow, their own agenda to pursue?

So often in your gospel, Jesus, those who presumed themselves to be the chosen ones came to be left outside, while those who hardly dared lift their face to look at you came to be the ones chosen. You cast down the mighty from their thrones and exalt the lowly.

But who are the lowly? That terrible word 'hypocrite', thrown around so lightly, its accusing finger always pointed at another, directed in judgment at those considered to be acting a part, is a double-edged blade: it cuts both ways. It is only God who knows the secrets of the human heart.

? *'Have you not read in the law that on the sabbath the priests in the*
• *temple break the sabbath and yet are guiltless?' (Matthew 12:5)*

I know what you are referring to, Jesus. The priests in the temple did heavy physical work on the sabbath, such as sacrificing animals, which would normally be forbidden. But because it was done for God, they were held to be guiltless.

Who wrote the law, Jesus? It did not all come from the finger of God on Mount Sinai. You said of those who sat on the chair of Moses, 'They tie up heavy burdens, hard to bear, and lay them on the shoulders of others; but they themselves are unwilling to lift a finger to move them.' That is close to the bone. How often Christian preaching laid on people's shoulders a burden of fear and guilt which became the motivator of their moral lives. We forgot that guilt was a good servant but a bad master. There are people for whom morals are a prison in which they have locked themselves, but bad moral teaching built the prison in the first place. By way of reaction, some have thrown out the baby with the bathwater and made the autonomous, self-assertive ego a caricature of conscience. We acted in ignorance, Jesus, and the prison we built imprisoned ourselves, too. Father, forgive us; we knew not what we did.

We find it hard to resist the temptation to reinforce every ideal with a law, to back up every principle with a sanction. Law appeals to the Pharisee in us; love we mistrust as vague, ill-defined and without content. Maybe that is because we have not experienced it. I think, Jesus, you meant law to be firstly an instrument of teaching, and only secondarily – if that – an instrument of control. The practitioners of the law switch those priorities. For you, law was a means of liberation, a help in our weakness, a stick to prevent stumbling, a light in the dark, a map for the road, a fence at the edge of the cliff.

In your eyes, the sabbath was made for the person, not the person for the sabbath. The law was made for the person, not the person for the law. You pointed out that if it was lawful to pull a sheep out of a pit on the sabbath, then surely, all the more, it was lawful to do good to a person on the sabbath. Everywhere and always the person. You said, 'Go and learn what this means: "I desire mercy, not sacrifice".' Love is the ultimate law. Its demands are greater and ask more than any law, but are light and energising to those who meet them, because they act out of love.

Jesus, Son of Man, you are lord of the sabbath. Thank you for rescuing it from legalism and rigidity, and making it an instrument of service, a day of rest, for humanity.

? *'If Satan casts out Satan, he is divided against himself; how then will his kingdom stand? If I cast out demons by Beelzebul, by whom do your own experts cast them out?' (Matthew 12:26-27)*

Jesus, they brought to you a man with a blind and dumb spirit, and you cast it out, healing him. The crowds were amazed but, amid the gasps of surprise and the shouts of joy, there were sneers of cynicism. They said you had done it by the power of Satan, of Beelzebul, and therefore you were a collaborator in evil.

How unhappily true to life! How bizarre, yet sad, that there are minds so cynical they will attribute an unworthy motive to any action, no matter how great or good. You responded by, in effect, inviting them to apply the test: 'Every good tree bears good fruit, but a bad tree bears bad fruit ... If it is by the finger of God that I cast out demons, then the Kingdom of God has come to you.' My actions speak for themselves so, if you don't believe my words, look at my actions and draw the appropriate conclusion.

Evil is a mystery, unfathomable. Why does a person choose it, will it, decide for it, knowingly and freely? And we do. I do. There is a hardness of heart which is resistant to good, which scoffs at it, belittles and disparages it, even to the point of self-destruction. The wilful, wrong-headed, stubborn refusal of good and choice of evil is what you meant, I think, Jesus, by blasphemy against the Holy Spirit. It is a sin which cannot be forgiven because the sinner refuses forgiveness, denies any need of it, spits with contempt on the very idea.

Jesus, your follower, Paul, wrote, 'Do not be overcome by evil but overcome evil with good.' You embodied that teaching. You were pro-active, not reactive. You followed your own agenda, not allowing others to determine it for you with their petty games of test and trick and trap. You slapped them down firmly when they tried those ploys.

For you, yes meant yes, and no meant no; you said what you meant and you meant what you said. Life is simpler that way.

You encountered seemingly endless opposition, Jesus. You were never free from the relentless, debilitating attentions of those who set out to disrupt and destroy. And they got you in the end. They finally succeeded. When you hung on the cross, they were still there, needling as before, 'He saved others; let him save himself ... Let him come down from the cross now, and we will believe in him.' You grieved at their hardness of heart, their blind perversity. But you welcomed the least sign of goodwill: 'Today you will be with me in paradise.' In your kingdom there is room for everyone; only those are excluded who have excluded themselves.

? *'You brood of vipers! How can you speak good things, when you are* **•** *evil?' (Matthew 12:34)*

The world that you moved in, Jesus, was one alive with manoeuvering for power. Among the contenders were the Pharisees: devout, intense, narrow, nationalistic, legalistic, traditionally-minded, serious laymen, close to the scribes.

Scribes: conscious of their status as the literate intelligentsia in contrast to manual labourers. Archivists, guardians of tradition. Systematisers who might have said 'Keep the rules and the rules will keep you.'

Sadducees: conservative landowners and merchants. Old money. They included many priests and aristocrats.

Priests: they represented the people to God and God to the people; they offered sacrifice and taught the law. They held power from within, controlling the spirit.

Pontius Pilate: Roman procurator of Palestine, he wanted to keep his patch quiet, collect the taxes, and maybe, with luck, get promoted out of his backwater. Cruel.

Herod Antipas, the one you called 'that fox'. A Jew in name more than in fact, he spied for the Emperor Tiberius on Pilate, who knew it and hated him for it, all the more so as he could do nothing about it. He lost his position when he was reported to Rome by his brother, Agrippa, whom he had been plotting to displace.

Those were the people among whom you found yourself, Jesus, truly a snake-pit of intrigue. Was it ever likely that among such competing factions you would find honest listening to your teaching and claims? Pilate was frank, with his dismissive, 'What is truth?' He saw your teaching as a matter of questions about words and names and the Jewish law, and he did not wish to be a judge of such matters; he paid no attention to any of those things.

You came with a new teaching – and it had authority. You rocked the boat, and that was bad politics. You could have been a success if you had been prepared to play the career game. But truth would have been the casualty.

You looked for people who cared for the truth and were prepared to commit themselves to it unreservedly. You want us to make a decision, to stop waiting to see which way the wind is blowing so that we can trim our sails accordingly. You want people who can speak the truth out of the abundance of their heart because they have submitted themselves to it, allowing it to seize and possess them in the knowledge that all truth, no matter how it is mediated, is of God.

? *'You of little faith, why did you doubt?' (Matthew 14:31)*

You ask why I doubt, Jesus. It is because I am human. God gave me a mind to think with. I live part-way between a sense of the presence and of the absence of God. Sometimes the sense of God's absence is more real. In our splintered, de-natured society, reduced to the level of functionaries, machine-minders, numbers and commuters, it is hard to see the face of God. But if there were no God, who would there be to thank for anything?

I do not feel ashamed of my doubts, Jesus. They help me to dig deeper, to get below the superficial answers that are an insult to your greatness. I need to experience doubt – desolation even – in order to live in depth and to find your image, not that of some idol. Unhappy are those who have never suffered the pain of doubt; they have not yet begun to live or find faith! You do not take away our sufferings, Jesus; you share them.

I come to the shore of faith only after I have travelled across the sea of doubt. I am often caught between faith and doubt; I have many unanswered questions, and I accept that most of them will remain unanswered. I ask why God allows the good to suffer, why I choose evil instead of good. But I know that if I try to measure God by the limitations of my mind I cannot but go wrong. God is not limited to my understanding of him; he is not made in my image and likeness. Like Peter, to whom you first put the question, Jesus, I get out of my depth and start to sink. You want me to sink into God and let go of my desire to be in control. When I surrender in trust I am upheld.

I do not have the impetuous courage of Peter who tried to walk to you on the water during a storm on the lake in the early morning. As long as he kept looking at you, he was safe. But when he noticed the strong wind, he became frightened, and began to sink. He cried out, 'Lord, save me!' and you immediately reached out your hand and caught him. He had left the security of the boat to venture onto the deep in response to your call. His companions must have thought him mad, as people do of anyone who ventures to risk all for God. But your message to us in our fears is: 'Take heart, it is I. do not be afraid!'

Doubt and faith are like two magnetic poles; they need each other. Without doubt, faith degenerates into gullibility; without faith, we never reach beyond ourselves. Doubt is necessary in order that we learn to trust. Thomas's doubts make our trust possible. May my doubts lead me to reverence, to say with Peter, 'Truly you are the Son of God.' May I believe so that I may understand. Then I will be able to venture on the impossible when you call me.

? *'Why do you break the commandment of God for the sake of your* **•** *tradition?' (Matthew 15:3)*

You were thinking, Jesus, of those in your time who dedicated their wealth to the temple, while continuing to live off its revenue. By doing so, they were declared free from the obligation to care for their elderly parents, because the wealth of the temple treasury was not to be put to 'profane' use.

Caring for parents was 'profane'? Whatever happened to the commandment of God, 'Honour your father and your mother'? You had hard words for such people: 'For the sake of your tradition, you make void the commandment of God.' And you went on, 'This people honours me with their lips, but their hearts are far from me; in vain do they worship me, teaching human precepts as doctrines.'

Sometimes I have the uneasy feeling, Jesus, that the moral teaching I learned showed me how to be tricky more than how to be moral. Wriggle-room was built into it, loopholes left in anticipation of future needs. We gave priority to consistency, precedent and upholding authority, though they were not priorities with you. You stated, 'You have heard that it was said … But I say to you …' You taught a teaching that was new – and with authority. Your authority was that you were the author. An author is an *auctor*, one who gives increase, who augments.

Some of what I learned, too, was human precepts being taught as divine doctrines. The mantra, 'The church teaches …' covered a multitude, some of it personal opinion which would later be dropped as an embarrassment. I think of what was said about matters such as capital punishment, slavery, usury, the use of the bible, biblical authorship, democracy, human rights and freedoms, church-state relations, colonialism, ecumenism, evolution, the dignity and role of women, the use of the vernacular in the liturgy, human sexuality, salvation outside the church and more. A lot of solemn and serious statements have been quietly swept under the carpet and allowed to die a natural death.

You tell us to focus on priorities – love of God and of neighbour. Maybe the question I should ask myself is, 'What would you, Jesus, do?' Is that not academic enough, too simplistic? We sometimes say it is, but perhaps what we really mean is that it asks too much. It is too radical and uncompromising in its simplicity.

? *'What do you think, Simon? From who do the kings of the earth take*
• *toll or tribute? From their children or others?' (Matthew 17:25)*

Jesus, this question of yours bothers me. Not the question itself, so
much as its context. The temple tribute you referred to was light, the
equivalent of two days' wages per year – nothing compared to
today's income tax. As a faithful, observant Jew you would have
paid it, in the same way that you usually went to the synagogue
each sabbath. Yet you speak here of the temple as if it were something alien, of which you were not a child. How could you think of
your Father's house as belonging to 'the kings of the earth'?

And then comes something even more puzzling. You say to
Peter, 'Go to the sea and cast a hook; take the first fish that comes up
and when you open its mouth, you will find a coin; take that, and
give it to them for you and for me.' This is the only instance in the
gospel where you performed a deed of power for your own benefit.
All other examples were for people in need. And yet you were not
destitute, nor even poor. You and your disciples were working men
with a trade. And the implication of what you say is that you recognised no obligation to pay the tribute, but did it so as not to give offence. That sounds like saying, 'Do it for form's sake to keep them
happy.' And that seems both to evade the issue of an obligation to
pay the tax, and to lack respect for the collectors.

Do you see my difficulty, Jesus? I cannot help but feel that this
story does not have the ring of truth about it. It seems out of harmony
with the rest of the gospel. You were never one to evade an issue, to
fob people off with a gesture, or to do something for the sake of a
quiet life. The story – forgive me, Jesus – sounds gimmicky.

Someone once wrote that we should read the gospel with a pen-
cil in our hands. When we agree with a passage, we should tick it
with a √, and thank God for it. When we do not understand something, we should put a question mark beside it, and try and find out
its meaning. When we disagree with something, we should mark it
with an x – and the xs point to the anti-Christ in us.

That last idea, Jesus, is hard-hitting and leaves me worried. Am I
placing myself in opposition to you because I have doubts about the
authenticity of this gospel story? I hope not. But there is something
not right about it.

You ask me questions, Jesus, not to get 'the right answer' but the
one I believe in. And I think you prefer honest dissent to dishonest
assent. Can we leave it at that for the moment? Maybe in the future I
will be able to see the matter in a better way.

? *'Who is the greatest in the kingdom of heaven?' (Matthew 18:1)*

You turn conventional values upside down, Jesus. If I – forgive my arrogance! – had ever been asked to design a religion, I would have shaped it in terms of the just use of power for human benefit. It would not have entered my head to think in your terms of the birth of a child in poverty and persecution, and his death in failure on a cross. You turn our wisdom upside down – and not without good reason.

The 'wise' men who came to Bethlehem at your birth – what was wise about them? They were so foolish as to pay a courtesy call on an unscrupulous murderer like King Herod and disclose their purpose to him, thereby bringing down slaughter on the innocents. Meanwhile the 'simple' shepherds got the message straight, acted on it, and found you.

The religious leaders of your country, the best and brightest of their people, were those from whom you had a right to expect support. Instead they were your most persistent opponents. They had a jewel in the palm of their hand and did not see it. You came to your own and they did not accept you. But those officially designated as 'sinners' by those same religious leaders recognised and welcomed you.

Pilate, with his flippant 'What is truth?' probably thought of himself as wise, mature, and experienced when, in reality, he was tired, negative, and cynical.

The Greek philosophers in the Areopagus, the intellectual leaders of their time, scoffed at the resurrection – what foolishness, they thought, when Paul told them of what he had seen on the road to Damascus.

You called a child, put him among your disciples, and said, 'Truly I tell you, unless you change and become like children, you will never enter the kingdom of heaven.' Your eyes were open to reality, Jesus. You must have been aware that children can lie, cheat, steal, bully, ridicule and be cruel, like the rest of us. You did not romanticise them or indulge in sentimentality. You must have had no illusions about their supposed docility: as every parent knows to the point of distraction, children never stop asking the question 'Why?' That is how they learn.

What you saw in children, Jesus, was their trusting dependence on their parents, their confidence that, whatever the problem, their parents can solve it. You want your followers to be child-like in their confident dependence on your Father. Your gospel is a declaration of dependence. Is that not complicated enough for me? Your servant, Thérèse, from Lisieux, knew better.

? *'What do you think? If a shepherd has a hundred sheep, and one of*
• *them has gone astray, does he not leave the ninety-nine on the*
mountains and go in search of the one that went astray?' (Matthew
18:12)

'What do you think?' Once again, Jesus, you are asking me to think
rather than supplying me with an answer. An answer discovered is
better than an answer supplied. It has greater impact and lasts
longer; a person 'owns' it. You did not spoon-feed people. You did
not break ideas down into sound bites and pour them into people's
heads. You drew people into the process of searching for the truth.
Once they learned the process, they could continue with it. If you
fed them with answers, they would always have to come back for
the next one. Give people a fish and you give them a meal; teach
them how to fish and you give them a lifetime of meals. You prod
us to think.

Jesus, I do not think I would have left the ninety-nine to go and
look for the one gone astray. I would have been afraid of losing the
ninety-nine, or some of them at least, while I was away. With regret
I would have accepted the loss of one for the sake of the rest. That
was not your way. But, of course, you were thinking of people, not
sheep. You treated people as individuals, not as 'the masses', a
'lumpen proletariat', an impersonal 'public' or 'them'. The person is
more important than people, said an Irish poet. Were you saying
that God never writes anyone off? How could a parent write off the
loss of a child?

You became the victim of a mind that said it was better to have
one person die, even if unjustly, for the people, than for the nation
to be put at risk. With that outlook, the person is reduced to the
level of an instrument, expendable. And if one is expendable, all are
expendable.

You were not a pragmatist, working on calculations of cost
effectiveness. You could not coldly regard the loss of a person as
regrettable-but-unavoidable. You were a universal lover, for whom
everyone matters. Underlying your refusal to accept such a loss was
your view of every person as a child of God your Father, created in
his image and likeness, and destined for eternal life with him. You
also had a vision, powered by hope, of what a person could become.
Where others saw problems you saw possibilities. Love believes all
things, hopes all things, endures all things.

? *Have you not read that the one who made them at the beginning*
• *'made them male and female,' and said, 'For this reason a man shall*
leave his father and mother and be joined to his wife, and the two
shall become one flesh'? (Matthew 19:4-6)

Yes, Jesus, I have read it. And I am glad that, from the beginning,
God made us male and female. He built relationships into our life
from the start; he made us complementary, mutually dependent. It
is not good for us to be alone; he made us for each other. In a word,
he made us need each other, perhaps so that we could learn our
need of him, learn that life is about interdependence.

I am glad, too, that our Father made us for each other, not only
spiritually, mentally or emotionally, but also bodily. He made the
human body the first sacrament. He made flesh grace-giving,
through the complementarity of our bodies, the two in one flesh.

Jesus, you also did so by yourself becoming flesh. The way you
showed us began with your birth as a child, saw you grow up
among a people, immersed in their life and culture. You were Jesus
of Nazareth. You walked among people, you let them touch you, you
fed them, you healed their bodies. And then you were killed, staked
like a hide to two pieces of wood. Your way is blood-and-gutsy,
neither ashamed of the flesh in its beauty and pleasure, nor in its
ugliness and pain.

Theologians have come to speak of your birth among us as 'in-
carnation', which is to say 'embodiment'. One of your followers
said we ought not to be ashamed to speak of what God was not
ashamed to create. Our faith is about flesh, bodies, sex, pain, suffering and death, and not only about ideas, mind, spirit, joy and heaven.
What God has joined together, let no one separate.

Sex, as God meant it from the beginning, speaks the language of
commitment, of a giving of self, the greatest gift – and irrevocable. It
was not meant to be 'Fuck around, fuck up and fuck off.' That is
hard-hearted. Or may I invent a word, and say 'dead-hearted'?

Our Father meant sex to be love-giving and life-giving, procre-
ative and unitive – in every sense, none excluded – an expression of
his inner life of mutuality, a giving and receiving of the self. Then
we reflect his image and likeness, in which we are made. Then we
are true to him and to ourselves, and do not play false to any person
or to nature. Then we are happy.

? *Have you never read, 'Out of the mouths of infants and nursing ba-*
• *bies you have prepared praise for yourself?' (Matthew 21:16)*

As every parent knows, Jesus, children can let the cat out of the bag, or the skeleton out of the cupboard, most embarrassingly. 'Mammy said ...' is sometimes the lead-in to a statement that can make Mammy cringe and wish she could disappear. I remember the children invited to compose prayers for a school assembly and one of them, in all simplicity, led off with 'Dear Jesus, please help Mammy and Daddy to stop fighting.' Blushes all round – except, of course, on the part of the child, who noticed nothing. I remember, too, the Catholic child, invited to share a prayer while attending a Jewish school in New York, who happily recited the Hail Mary!

Children let it out; they mention the unmentionable. With them there is no rehearsal, no self-censorship, no striving for effect, no thought of possible reaction – it just comes out. They announce for all the world to hear that the king's new clothes are no clothes at all, just nakedness.

A child's assessment can be devastating in its accuracy and shocking in its directness – and all the more since it was not calcul-ated to hit or hurt, just a candid statement of how it seems. In the mid-thirties, Winston Churchill, in the political wilderness and suf-fering from depression, was asked by two boys working on a school assignment, 'Now that you are old and retired, how do you pass the time?' There is no reply that can be made; all a person can do is keep the mouth shut and bear the mortification.

The gospel says, Jesus, that when you entered Jerusalem at the climax of your mission, the children cried out in the temple in praise of you, 'Hosanna to the Son of David!' The chief priests and the scribes became angry, but you answered them with your question. The children shouted what they saw and no one could stop them. They saw with the clear eyes of the innocent, for whom the political manoeuvres of the day are meaningless, who are unaware of the social pitfalls, or of the lies that adults tell. They told it like it was, the simple unvarnished truth. Bless them for it!

You taught us to say what we mean and mean what we say: 'Let your yes be yes and your no be no.'

> **?** *What do you think? A man had two sons; he went to the first and*
> *said, 'Son, go and work in the vineyard today.' He answered, 'I will*
> *not'; but later he changed his mind and went. The father went to the*
> *second and said the same; and he answered, 'I go, sir'; but he did not*
> *go. Which of the two did the will of the father?' (Matthew 21:28-32)*

Jesus, you said, 'Truly, I tell you, the tax collectors and the prostitutes are going into the kingdom of God ahead of you. For John
came to you in the way of righteousness and you did not believe
him, but the tax collectors and the prostitutes believed him; and even
after you saw it, you did not change your minds and believe him.'

You contrasted those who initially rejected the law of God – the
tax collectors and the prostitutes – but came to repentance through
the preaching of John the Baptist, with the official teachers of the
law of God – the chief priests and elders – who claimed to do God's
will but did not. And even the conversion of the tax collectors and
prostitutes did not persuade them.

Why did the chief priests and elders reject first John and then
you? The issue, to which your parable was a reply, was authority.
They would not accept you because you operated outside their system. No rabbi had imposed hands on you, designating you as his
successor. You pointed to a higher teaching authority, the authority
of truth that comes from God. But that bypassed their system. It
wasn't institutional or hierarchical and, for them, that was an obstacle
they could not get over.

You said this with your local situation in mind. But it is not very
different today, except in details of circumstance. There is always a
thorny relationship between the professional and the amateur, the
priest and the prophet, those within and without an institutional,
hierarchical structure. There is a world of difference between declaring that something is true because the authorities say it is, and
the authorities declaring it because it is true.

One day your disciples came back to you saying that someone
had been casting out demons in your name, and they had tried to
stop him, because he did not follow with them. You replied, 'Do not
stop him; for whoever is not against you is for you.'

One group was self-enclosed in a cocoon of complacent certitudes. The others were open to listen, to learn, to change. Where this
is concerned, Jesus, may I not look at others, thinking, 'If the cap
fits, wear it!', but ask myself in truth whether it fits me. The word
'disciple' means a learner.

> ? Woe to you, blind guides, who say, 'Whoever swears by the sanctuary
> • is bound by nothing, but whoever swears by the gold of the sanctuary
> is bound by the oath.' You blind fools! Which is greater, the gold, or
> the sanctuary that has made the gold sacred? (Matthew 23:17)

The pedantic casuistry engaged in by religious leaders in your time, Jesus, was an obstacle to people's growth towards God. The leaders said, for instance, that if a person swore an oath on the law, it was invalid; but the same oath, sworn on what was written in the law, was valid. Such distinctions leave me confused and cold, delightful though they are to some. What good purpose does such hair-splitting serve? No wonder you held them up as examples of what not to do!

I think, Jesus, your essential point was that only God is holy; there are no holy places, things or people. You said, 'No one is good but God alone.' There is only one absolute – God – and all else is relative. How true it is that institutions and structures, laws and teachings, put in place to be God-serving and gospel-serving sometimes become self-serving. If a church or any community of faith becomes more concerned for itself, its structures and traditions, its stability and continuity or, even worse, its public image, than for the people or the gospel it exists to serve, then it has fallen into idolatry, the temptation you rejected in the desert. 'No one,' you said, 'can serve two masters ...'

If we, through internal wrangles and preoccupations, turn inwards, we lose sight of those whom the institution was meant to serve, and maintenance takes over from mission. The church, for example, is not an end in itself. It is there to serve the kingdom, God's community. If it becomes self-serving instead of gospel-serving then it is an obstacle to grace, in strict terms, a scandal.

The church exists for the 'outsiders'; they are its *raison d'être*. The question people sometimes ask, 'Will the church survive?' is unanswerable, since it relates to a future of which we can know nothing. But, in any event, it misses the essential. The survival of the church is not the point. You did not die on the cross to ensure the survival of the church (if such a term as 'church' can be applied to the community of disciples you called into being.) You died so as to gather into one the dispersed children of God. What matters is whether the church, here and now, is fulfilling the mission you gave it. If it is, it will survive; if not, it won't, nor deserve to, unless it is converted. The church is always in need of reformation, and never more so than when, in surprise, it asks, 'Whatever do you mean?'

? *'You snakes, you brood of vipers! How can you escape being sentenced to hell?' (Matthew 23:33)*

It makes me laugh, Jesus, to hear people at times speak foolishly and naïvely of religion as a soother, a security wrap. You declare us to be a bunch of snakes – is that what people call a comfort blanket? I am asked how I can expect to escape being sentenced to hell – am I supposed to find that re-assuring?

This whole chapter 23 of your gospel writer, Matthew, was written for religious professionals of whatever stripe or grade. And how it stings! It forces us to acknowledge that the scribes and Pharisees are far from dead; they are alive and well, and their spirit rules in us. Indeed what the law was to the Pharisees, the church has become to us.

We have not learned what you sought to teach, Jesus. Why? We resist learning; we are afraid to trust people, afraid of losing control, afraid that things will get out of hand if we do not keep a tight grip on the reins. We have a bagful of clichés to justify this, tired stale catch-phrases like 'Better safe than sorry'. We parody the Christian virtue of prudence: instead of a guide for action, we make it a substitute for action, or an excuse for inaction.

We misuse language: when we exercise power we call it service; we demand control and call it *communio*. When the Spirit breathes where it wills, we frown and speak of the dangers of subjectivism and individualism. (What of the dangers of objectivism and communism? The twentieth century saw both in plenty.) Misused language always takes its revenge; language is not a toy to play with. Having misused it, we will call on it in our need and find it empty, without the bell-ring of truth, only a rattle that arouses no one.

We are afraid to trust people and even to trust you, Jesus, unless you confine yourself to what we call the tried and trusted paths of the past, unless you stay within the system. And that past we look at through tinted glasses, seeing only what we want to see, imagining some mythical good old days when people really had the faith. Our nostalgia for the past provides no meaning for the present or agenda for the future, and our efforts to re-claim it are sterile and wasteful.

Sear us, Jesus, now rather than later. Burn us with the blush of shame for our timidity. Cauterise our self-inflicted wounds of dullness and stupidity; they were our security wrap. Tear it away and throw it in the fire. Wake us up, Jesus, bring us back to life; we need your fire, the fire of life.

? *'Who, then, is the faithful and wise slave, whom his master has put
in charge of his household, to give the other slaves their allowance of
food at the proper time?' (Matthew 24:45)*

You had just spoken, Jesus, of vigilance and wakefulness. You want
us to be aware and awake, alert and alive to what is happening –
and to do our job. You don't want us to day-dream our way
through life, to be like Emmanuel in *Fawlty Towers* whose answer to
every question of accountability was 'Me, I know nothing!'

Adolf Hitler, in his autobiography, *Mein Kampf*, made clear his
hatred of Jews and contempt of Slavs. It was published in 1927, fif-
teen years before the Wannsee conference that instituted the death
camps. A copy was given to every German soldier, in place of the
bible. The German people said they did not know. Dachau concen-
tration camp, near the German city of Munich, opened for its cruel
business three weeks after Hitler came to power in 1933. The
German people said they did not know. Were the German people a
nation of racist thugs with a penchant for mass murder? I do not believe it. But they placed their destiny in the hands of a man who, in
their name, carried out the largest, most systematic genocide in
human history. They said they did not know, that they were unaware
of it.

Are the people of Ireland, Britain and the USA corrupt? I do not
believe it. They are mostly decent, honest people. But such people
have a way of allowing corruption to be carried on in their name.
Edmund Burke, an Irish parliamentarian, wrote, 'Nothing is required for the triumph of evil save that the good do nothing.' When
challenged, decent, honest people often say they did not know,
even after they have re-elected politicians whose corruption or
criminality had been publicly exposed before the election. Whether
that was because they did not care, or they did not want to know
and lacked the moral courage to face the challenge, only they can
say.

Jesus, you said, 'The slave who knew what his master wanted,
but did not prepare himself or do what he wanted, will receive a
severe beating. From everyone to whom much has been given,
much will be required; and from the one to whom much has been
entrusted, even more will be demanded.' So much for the 'consola-
tions' of religion, or its being a form of wish-fulfilment! You are saying bluntly, 'Wake up, face your responsibilities, and do your
work!' That is nothing if not clear and demanding.

? *Do you think that I cannot appeal to my Father, and he will at once send me more than twelve legions of angels? But how, then, would the scriptures be fulfilled, which say that it must happen in this way? (Matthew 26:53-54)*

I think, Jesus, that you are re-stating here your commitment to the way of humanity. You renounce any short-cuts or quick fixes. Your priority always was your Father and his rule, reign or kingdom, nothing else. And your way to that was by means of your humanity; you would not pull rank and claim the rights you were entitled to as the only-begotten son of God. Although you were in the form of God, you did not regard equality with God as something to be exploited, but you emptied yourself, taking the form of a slave, being born in human likeness. And you humbled yourself and became obedient to the point of death – even death on a cross.

You had already made that commitment at the start of your public life when, in the desert, you rejected the temptations of Satan, in which he called on you to renounce your humanity and assert the power of your divinity. You do the same again now, close to the end of your life. You were unambiguous in living by your commitment to the way of humanity, which is the way of suffering. You entered into our suffering. That suffering is a mystery, and you chose, not to explain it, but to share it. You do not renege on your promises, you are faithful to them. You were human through and through, and you would not cheat on that, even in the extremity of your suffering, by calling on your Father for help.

I am suspicious of those private revelations that come along from time to time claiming to offer an insider's view, a sneak preview, so to speak, of the mind of God. They lay claim to hidden knowledge of the will of God, and they make forecasts – nearly always gloomy – about the future, unless people do this or that. These exercises in religious voyeurism leave me cold. They do not fit. They jar with what you said about how you became one like us in all things, except sin. You came for all, not for a privileged few with some secret knowledge undisclosed to others. You shared our condition, including its ignorance. Nothing human was alien to you.

I do not wish, Jesus, to do anything other than walk the common path of humanity, with all that that implies. I am happy to live with uncertainty, ambiguity and paradox. I am not asking for the veil to be drawn aside for me to peep into the Holy of Holies. The more human I become, the more I fulfil my vocation; the more human I become, the more divine I become. Humanity is your road to divinity, and mine, too, as far as I am able.

? *'Why were you searching for me? Did you not know that I must be in my Father's house?' (Luke 2:49)*

I know, Jesus, of a friar-artist who was invited to paint a mural, depicting you, behind the altar in the sanctuary of a church in Nicaragua. Because the wall was large, the friar asked that the church be closed so he could have a free hand to bring the project to completion without interruption.

The day came when the task was done, the people came for Sunday Mass in the church and, of course, the mural was on view for the first time. The friar, dressed in civvies, mingled with the crowd after Mass and listened for reactions. It did not take him long to realise that they did not like it. They said your figure, Jesus, was too ordinary looking, too much like one of themselves – in fact, just like someone you would meet as you walked down the road. You were depicted like the men of the country, short, stocky, with yellowish skin and black hair, and dressed in shirt and trousers. They felt the mural should have shown you as tall, slim, white-skinned, fair-haired, with blue eyes, dressed in a flowing, white garment, and gazing off into eternity, absorbed in the contemplation of some heavenly mystery.

What those people wanted was a Jesus of Hollywood, the gospel according to Cecil B. De Mille. They could not accept your humanity, any more than the people of Nazareth did when they asked, 'Is not this the carpenter, the son of Mary? Where did this man get all this?' In effect, they were saying that you were just one of them, so you could not be any good.

If the mural in Nicaragua had shed tears, people would have flocked in droves to see it. If you had worked miracles in Nazareth every week, you would have been the most popular man in town. But you were ordinary and human, so they could not accept you. From Nicaragua to Nazareth to any ordinary town, we make our prophets demi-gods. By divinising you at the expense of your humanity, we keep you at a distance, Jesus, safely up on a pedestal. But your humanity brings you down to earth; it challenges us; you are one of us and we have to relate to you. Sometimes we do not want that. We say, 'Leave me alone; I'm OK as I am.' But you were never one to let sleeping dogs lie.

Where should I expect to find you? You are always doing your Father's business, in the ordinary affairs of human life, especially among the poor, the downtrodden and the outcasts.

? *Why do you call me 'Lord, Lord,' and not do what I tell you? (Luke 6:46)*

Your way, Jesus, is a way of action, a way of living and of loving. It is never simply a way of knowledge. That way may be open to only a few, but the way of love is open to all. One of your faithful followers, Bonaventure, wrote that even the simplest, most unlettered person can love God more than the most learned theologian – and he was no mean theologian himself. The authentic sign of Christian living is love, the kind that shows itself in sacrifice and self-giving, and which perseveres through thick and thin, not baulking at the cost in suffering.

Your way, Jesus, was to do your Father's will in all things. You lived for him, not for yourself. You said that you came down from heaven, not to do your own will, but the will of him who sent you. And that was no empty promise. When the moment of choice came, the decisive life-or-death choice in the garden of Gethsemane and on the hill of Calvary, you fulfilled your promise. You gave your life to the full, holding nothing back.

Jesus, is it any wonder that I hold back, that I am frightened at the intensity of such self-giving? I do indeed say, 'Lord, Lord', I say it in prayers every day. But I do not do what you tell me, that is true. I cling to the self, afraid to let go, fearful of taking the plunge and accepting in my heart that to let go of self is to let God take me to himself. In prayer as in life there are always the two poles: the movement inwards to self and then the movement outwards to God. About this, let me not say, 'I cannot' if the truth is 'I will not'.

What holds me back is not a problem in my intellect that calls for a solution in new ideas or fresh understanding; it is an obstacle in the will called sin, the love of self that over-rides love of the other, or the Other. The danger in my prayer, as in my life, is to remain locked in my self, to look for the gifts of God rather than the God of gifts, to want experiences, to search for them in techniques. The only technique a Christian has or needs is love.

Prayer and its fruits, which seem to start from my efforts, are in reality always a gift of God. Let me be content to start by doing what I can, no matter how humiliatingly inadequate it is. Let me pray as I can, not as I can't, as one of your servants advised. And may I remember, too, that the best kind of prayer is that in which there is most love.

? *'To what then will I compare the people of this generation, and what*
• *are they like?' (Luke 7:31)*

You posed this rhetorical question, Jesus, in frustration. You saw
that when John the Baptist came urging fasting and repentance,
some people – usually the leaders and teachers of the law – said he
was a fanatic. But when you came eating and drinking and preaching of God's merciful love, the same people said you were a friend
of sinners, with the insinuation that you were permissive towards
sin. Your critics were habitual fault-finders, people who would neither pull nor push, neither lead nor be led, those who would not see
the doughnut but only the hole in the middle.

Your complaint about their capriciousness was understandable.
They were indeed like the children in the marketplace that you
spoke of: if someone played the flute for them, they would not
dance; if someone sang a sad song for them, they would not cry.
One way or the other, they would not play the game.

The situation has not changed, Jesus. In all of us – including myself – there is a longing for freedom, but an unwillingness to accept
its undesired consequences. We want to be free; we always have.
But we want you to intervene when our exercise of freedom goes
wrong. Evil is the product of the misuse of human freedom. But
when we see evil we say, 'If God is all-knowing, loving and powerful, why does he not intervene to prevent evil in the world?' We
want rights, but baulk at the accompanying responsibilities.

There is a psychologist, Jesus, in our time – they weren't around
in yours, at least not formally – who says that the average believer
lives at a mental age of eight, and the average unbeliever at a mental
age of three. We are indeed at times like children, swinging from
one extreme to another, not knowing what we want, petulantly demanding this or that, only to fling it away when given it.

But there were some who listened to you, Jesus. They were those
who were aware of their sinfulness; they did not seek to trivialise
the idea of sin or to explain it away; they did not deny or justify
their wrongdoing. They were not afraid to speak the words, 'I was
wrong.' And they are with us today, too. They are those whom you
called the poor in spirit, those who know their need of God, who are
open to hear you in their hearts, who know they have a long way to
go but make an effort to get there. Alone of all people, you said of
the poor in spirit, 'Theirs is the kingdom of heaven'. Not 'will be',
but 'is'. Thank you, Jesus. You give me hope.

? *'Who touched me?' (Luke 8:45)*

Jesus, you were in the middle of a large crowd which pressed in on you, and you asked the question 'Who touched me?' No wonder your followers were surprised; everybody was touching you.

A woman had said to herself, 'If I but touch his clothes, I will be made well.' Her touch, since she suffered from a haemorrhage, made you ritually unclean in terms of Jewish law. You made no objection to that, saying only to her, 'Your faith has made you well; go in peace, and be healed of your illness.' And she was.

There are touches and touches. They range from insignificant to highly significant. They can mediate gentleness, desire, correction, anger or love; they can draw attention. Even an infant can tell the difference: washing a baby is not like washing a plate. Touches can be grace-giving, like the anointings in baptism, confirmation, orders, and the care of the sick. They can herald a moment of conversion, like Francis of Assisi hugging and kissing the leper whose appearance frightened and disgusted him, thereby embracing and healing what he feared in himself.

People like to touch things, especially things associated with the high and mighty: the memorabilia of Jacqueline Kennedy, Princess Diana, and Elvis Presley, or Bono's shades, the relics of the great and the good. Half of Ireland went to see and touch the relics of Thérèse of Lisieux. People like to kiss the cross on Good Friday, and even those who rarely come to a church come on Ash Wednesday for the ashes. It is the touch, the direct contact between one person and another, that counts.

It was the same, Jesus, with your servant, Paul. God did extraordinary things through him, so that when the handkerchiefs or aprons that had touched his skin were brought to the sick, their diseases left them, and the evil spirits came out of them.

Jesus, you stretched out your hand and touched a leper, the untouchable, healing him. You laid hands on people, a gesture that signified forgiveness or their being sent out on a mission. Your followers were proud to be able to say that they had seen you with their eyes and touched you with their hands.

But you also said, 'Do not hold on to me.' To be touched is not to be grabbed, clung to, or possessed by a dependence that refuses to grow up. You gave a hand-up rather than a hand-out.

? *'You fools! Did not the one who made the outside [of the cup] make the inside also?' (Luke 11:40)*

Once again, Jesus, you were at a meal. You received lots of invitations and you accepted them. The Pharisee who invited you was amazed to see that you did not first wash before dinner; this was a requirement, one of the social graces of polite society. We, likewise, fuss about details, about holding the knife and fork correctly, knowing when to use which item of cutlery, the difference between a serviette and a napkin. To use a fork the wrong way up, to tip the soup plate towards you instead of away from you – people feel horror at the thought that they might commit a *faux pas* that violates these *de rigueur* demands of gracious living. But the rules of the table have meaning only insofar as they express respect or kindness towards one's fellow diners, no more.

You call us to a sense of priorities. How often we get the details right and miss the essentials. You spoke of those who clean the outside of the cup and of the dish, but inside are full of greed and wickedness. No wonder you called us fools! You call on us to clean the heart as well as the cup and dish, the heart which is the source of good and evil. Cleaning the dishes while leaving uncleansed a heart that is full of greed and wickedness is the kind of foolish and misdirected priority that we are good at.

Why did you speak in particular of greed? You said, 'Give for alms those things that are within; and see, everything will be clean for you.' The things that are within, and which we need to give up, include evil attitudes and habits, such as greed or selfishness. You are saying, Jesus, that inner purification must be practical. Almsgiving is a test of this; otherwise it may be just talk or theory, less than honest ways of keeping at bay the challenge of coming to a decision and moving into action. The simple challenge to part with some money is clear-cut and direct. It is a real and vivid test of whether my pledge to following you goes beyond wishful thinking.

You showed, Jesus, that you knew us because, even in this matter, you held out, to entice us, the prospect of a reward. We take persuading. You said, 'Everything will be clean for you.' If I am clean within, then the outside will also be clean. If I can give of my money, then I will be able to give of myself. Generosity evokes generosity, and meanness meanness – that I have seen many times. I remember a confrère who was a most generous, self-giving man; people practically tripped over each other to give him help because they knew he would pass it on to those in need, holding back nothing for himself. He had his priorities right.

? *'Friend, who has set me as judge or arbitrator over you?' (Luke*
• *12:14)*

Jesus, a man in the crowd had said to you, 'Teacher, tell my brother to divide the family inheritance with me.' He had paid you a compliment, bestowing on you the title of 'Teacher'. It meant you had 'arrived'; you had status in the community. It was natural that he should ask you to act as arbitrator in his dispute. You replied to him with your question and went no further with it.

You called him a friend. Our friends are not so much those who are nice to us – what a vacuous word 'nice' is! – as those who will what is for our good, who, for example, tell us the truth about ourselves even when we do not want to hear it. I notice, Jesus, that nowhere in the gospel did you tell us to be nice to each other. That is a relief. You told us to love one another, and that ranges further, digs deeper and costs more than any amount of being nice.

You were not 'nice' to the Pharisees when you called them hypocrites, or a bunch of snakes. I cannot imagine that they liked it. But it was for their good; it was necessary that you break through the hard carapace of their complacency so as to create the possibility that they open up to truth. Deliberately to leave a person in untruth or ignorance is no kindness, but an act of despair, or possibly of contempt. It suggests, 'Why bother? There's no point in wasting time on him.' Deliberately to leave a child uncorrected, for instance, taking the line of least resistance and calling it kindness, is acting out a lie. You said, Jesus, 'The truth will make you free.' Better a discomfiting truth than either a comforting half-truth or a consoling lie.

Love is not selective; to love one is to love all. To hate one is to hate all. Love is being able to say, 'I don't like Joe or Ann – that is the truth. But, despite that, I respect them because they are creatures of God like me; I will do what is for their good, act towards them with justice, build them up in any way I can, and pray to God for them.' That goes further and demands more than the niceties of social convention, that cluster of ambiguities which can mask even hatred.

I am sure, Jesus, that the man in the crowd was disappointed with you. He had wanted you to intervene, to summon his brother and authoritatively insist on a just settlement. You did not do it. You left him to solve the problem himself. I do not think you did for people what they were able to do for themselves, using the gifts you had already given them. To do that is an untruth; it belittles a person.

? *'Can any of you by worrying add a single hour to your span of life? If then you are not able to do so small a thing as that, why do you worry about the rest?' (Luke 12:26)*

Yes, Jesus, we worry. There are people who are not happy unless they are worrying. They would worry about a fly walking up a wall. They make a crisis out of everything, and if they do not find one, they create one. They do not like problems, they want disasters.

We do not trip over mountains, but over mole-hills. I remember the woman in Africa who had been attacked and badly injured by a crocodile. At least that is what she said – but that is another story. She was lucky to have escaped – not many do. When I was bringing her to hospital by truck, and looked at her torn flesh visible through the rends in her blood-stained clothes, my concern was to get her there before she died. But her concern was, 'Where's my snuff-box?' She had lost it in the river and was in a great tizzy until someone gave her a cigarette instead.

Germany's Otto von Bismarck, the driving force behind the creation of a united German Empire in the nineteenth century, was a different man at home. The Iron Chancellor would stand at the head of the dinner table in the evening, watch in hand, checking to see that the dinner began on time. If it was delayed, even by one minute, he sometimes would reduce himself to tears in a temper tantrum, bemoaning the decline in standards. Some highly intelligent adults can be more childish than a child.

I think your point, Jesus, was about people who worry about trivia. What would they do in a real crisis? Every pain is bearable – except the one I've got. And, of course, most of our problems are DIY jobs, self-inflicted. Many of the things we worried about, if we looked back on them later on, never came to anything, and we were foolish to have worried about them in the first place.

I think you want me to take one day at a time, and to live this day today. That way I live fully. I do not want to spend the week waiting for the weekend, the year waiting for the holidays, my working life waiting for retirement, and retirement waiting for death. I do not want to live with one eye on the past, the other on the future, and none left for the present, so that I lose the gift it represents. I believe in the sacrament of the present moment. Each day is a new page of the gospel that you write for us. To live in the present is to live simply, more completely, more humanly, in a less taxing manner, truly living life, not just passing through it. The present is the only time in which I can truly live.

? *'Do you think I have come to bring peace to the earth?'* (Luke 12:51)

Yes, Jesus, I did. I had hoped that your coming on earth would bring peace. Did Isaiah not speak of you as the Prince of Peace? Was it not your mission to reconcile us to God and then give us the ministry of reconciliation? Am I naïve or unrealistic to hope?

I live in a divided world, and its divisions start with me; I live in a divided self. I know, too, that there is division in individuals, families, communities, workplaces, nations and internationally. I do not mean only diversity or difference, but real division that sets people against each other. It seems that we humans have an innate propensity to divide.

What particularly troubles me, Jesus, is that, in human history, religion was often the excuse, the occasion, or even the cause of division. I know that so-called 'religious' wars had as their motivating force political, social, economic, cultural, dynastic or personal considerations. But religion was sometimes there, too, providing the moral ammunition, stoking the fires of anger and hatred, even to the ultimate betrayal, the attempt to co-opt God to one's own side.

You were an intense person, Jesus; you had a sense of urgency, of the need to make a decision, a choice, a commitment. For you, the totality of your awareness of God your Father was such that you would not give him less than everything, and you call on us to do likewise. You were not one for hedging your bets; you did not want people to be neither hot nor cold, but lukewarm. You came to bring fire, not sedatives, to the earth. Your language was not one of bland platitudes; you were not afraid of the risk of causing offence; you were a sign of contradiction to your people. This sense of urgency made you impatient with half-measures, with people who wanted to have the best of all worlds. You even said you had come to bring division, and you underlined that point saying, 'Whoever loves father or mother more than me is not worthy of me; whoever does not take up the cross and follow me is not worthy of me. Those who find their life will lose it, and those who lose their life for my sake will find it.'

Jesus, I do not wish to draw the teeth of those powerful statements, to dilute them by clever ambiguities or casuistic subtleties. You want me to commit myself to you without equivocation, making war on anything, especially in myself, that separates me from you. The peace I had hoped for was, I think, the peace of a quiet life, a cushy cruise with no demands, no hard sayings, no difficult choices. You ask me for nothing less than all.

? *'You hypocrites! You know how to interpret the appearance of earth and sky, but why do you not know how to interpret the present time?' (Luke 12:56)*

Like many farming peoples, the Jews of your time, Jesus, knew how to read the signs of a change in the weather. They knew that wind from the south-west meant rain, while from the south-east it was the sirocco, the hot, dust-laden and oppressive wind from the desert. Probably every culture has similar knowledge of weather patterns, and folklore around them expressed in rhyme, saying and song. The sayings are usually accurate, too, even if they describe signs which do not usually give much advance warning.

You complained to the people, Jesus, that while they were able to recognise signs in the earth and the sky, they were unable to interpret their own time. Probably like ourselves, though to a greater degree in our agitated world of the twenty-first century, your people were so occupied with the daily routine that, in practical terms, they were unable to stand back and think about the direction in which life, especially their life, was moving. They could not see the wood for the trees. How many Europeans today have anything more than the haziest idea of the wars in the Balkans in the nineties, wars that killed 250,000 people and created two million refugees, and were reported daily in the mass media?

The poet said, 'Human kind cannot bear very much reality.' It is true. We live far from ourselves, we spend our lives running away from ourselves, and we barter the truth for trifles. Especially we spend our life running away from the source and foundation of life which is God. Man's search for God, as an Irish Christian apologist remarked, is like the mouse's search for the cat. There is tension in us between a self-centred life and one that is God-centred. We habitually choose the former, and it is natural to us to do so. Yet our orientation is to God, like a compass needle's is to the north.

I think, Jesus, that we run away from God out of fear of what he might ask. He might ask what we do not wish to give. And, by our lights, we are right, because God asks for everything. He has told us that he is a jealous God who will settle for nothing less than totality. He does not want us to keep even a tiny little corner for ourselves. He unashamedly wants all. He is entitled to it, since it is his anyway, and we can truly claim nothing for ourselves, except our sins. But God is a lover, not a rapist. His embrace is freeing and upbuilding, not stifling or destructive. He courts and invites and is prepared to wait until we are ready to surrender in love – with the pain and sacrifice that love entails.

? *'Why do you not judge for yourselves what is right?' (Luke 12:57)*

Once again, Jesus, a wake-up call, a call to conscience. You are telling me to switch on my head and think. Pretty often, I would prefer not to. I am like the person in the film who said, 'When I works, I works hard, but when I thinks, I falls asleep.' But, if thinking is demanding work, which it is, neither do I want someone else to do my thinking for me or, even less, to allow clichés and half-baked slogans become a substitute for thinking.

Conscience is an unremitting search for the truth with a commitment to following it when found. It is the servant of truth, and truth is of God. I wish to have an active, well-developed conscience. This is my right and responsibility as a human being.

I know that the development of conscience is a matter more of will than of intellect, more of choice than of understanding. I know from my sinfulness, an ever-present teacher, that my conscience in great matters has been dulled and rendered insensitive by repeated infidelities in small matters. But, Jesus, you said, 'They who are faithful in that which is little are faithful also in that which is great.' I know that I cannot quench my conscience one moment and expect it to shine like a light the next.

Language has changed and, in consequence, ideas and actions. Where we used to talk about sin we began to speak of deviance; from deviance we changed to preference; from preference to choice; and from choice to freedom. It is as if we claim that we ought to be – or are – free to commit sin, and have a right to do so, whereas the truth is that we have a right and a duty to do good and avoid evil.

I am tempted by a superficial, Coca-Cola psychology which suggests that guilt feelings are neurotic, though they are to conscience what pain is to the body – an alarm-call for self-examination. I am influenced by the notion that equates conscience with 'doing your own thing' in the name of personal freedom, though subject to every fashion or fad. That is arbitrary, selective, and individualistic; it undermines common values and a sense of community. Jesus, a follower of yours wrote, 'Conscience is a stern monitor, but it has been superseded by a counterfeit, which the centuries prior to it never heard of, and could not have mistaken for it if they had. It is the right of self-will.'

Conscience makes us mature human beings, responsible and accountable, without self-deception. It is a demand of our humanity. It makes for good relationships, good health of soul, mind and body. It is your voice in me, Jesus. Seeking it, may I find it; finding it, may I follow it. Happiness is joy in the truth.

? 'At that very time there were some present who told him about the
• Galileans whose blood Pilate had mingled with their sacrifices. He
asked them, 'Do you think that because these Galileans suffered in
this way they were worse sinners than all other Galileans? Or the
eighteen who were killed when the tower of Siloam fell on them – do
you think that they were worse offenders than all the others living in
Jerusalem?'' (Luke 13:1-2, 4)

Suffering is a mystery, and many people from Job to yourself, Jesus,
have wrestled with it. The simple idea that suffering is caused by
sin, or is God's punishment for it, is untenable. It is shallow, simplistic and perhaps unjust. But it is not entirely without truth.

Some suffering is caused by sin: repeated lying, cheating, or
breaking promises, undermine trust, and that brings suffering. But
it is suffering that I bring on myself. I cannot blame God or anyone
else for it. The Greeks used to say that virtue is its own reward; they
had a point. Perhaps vice is its own punishment.

The effects of sin can pass from generation to generation. One
can see this in societies such as Rwanda, the Balkans and Northern
Ireland, where cycles of aggression and revenge, attack and
counter attack, between one community and another are perpetuated
through myth and folklore, drawing each new generation into a
fresh spiral of hate, a harsh reminder that actions have consequences. The spiral continues until someone breaks it by a prophetic
act of forgiveness.

Where was God in the suffering in the United States on 11th
September 2001? God was where people put him – out of their lives.
That remains true, even though those responsible rejoiced to claim
that they acted in God's name, on his behalf. To do wrong in the
name of God is blasphemy. The hatred which filled the attackers
was a sin, and it brought in its train a huge toll of suffering. That
suffering was a judgment on the attackers, not on their victims.

But suffering can be redemptive, it can purify, it can strip us
down to essentials, tearing away the masks of falsity and pretence
that we hide behind, revealing to us the truth about ourselves – perhaps for the first time. If God wishes to build a cathedral in the soul,
he has first to clear away the accumulated debris until he reaches
the foundation of rock. If there was ever a person who never suffered, that person is one to be pitied, living on the surface of life in a
kind of Disneyland where the sky is always blue and the grass is always green.

Most human suffering is caused by people, and can be prevented
or remedied by them, using the means God has given. 'Thy will be
done' is not only a plea but a commitment.

? *'What is the kingdom of God like? And to what should I compare it?' (Luke 13:18)*

I hope you are not depending on me, Jesus, for an answer to this question. You already know what the kingdom of God is since you are its King, and you are also the master of parables. All I know is that your kingdom is not like any earthly kingdom; it was you who said, 'My kingdom is not from this world.' Maybe the kingdom means the world as you would like it to be.

Two mothers lived on the same street, and their sons were close friends from childhood. Then something happened that divided the young men. Was it a row over a girl? Perhaps. One evening they met by chance after both of them had had 'a few drinks', that is to say, a lot of drink. They quarrelled, lost their tempers, then one pulled out a knife and stabbed the other. Luckily, there were people near them who pulled them apart before too much harm was done. But the injured man had to be brought to hospital for stitches to a light stab wound. He was discharged after a short while.

Later that night they met again, this time with more drink taken. The same young man pulled his knife out again and stabbed the other once more, this time killing him. The police were called and the attacker was arrested and brought away. The news spread along the street like a shock wave, hitting the two families very hard.

The next day the mother of the dead man visited the mother of his killer. She said to her, 'We have both lost a son. My son is dead, and when your son is out of jail, he will be a different person.' They threw their arms around each other in an embrace of shared suffering.

Talking to her local priest about it afterwards, the victim's mother said, 'I am not a good Catholic. I do not go to Mass every Sunday, but I know that when I die I will have to ask God for forgiveness for a lot of things, and I could not do that if I was not ready to forgive.' Her attitude was as simple and direct as that.

Will you accept that true story of reconciliation, Jesus, as my contribution to your search for a parable of how the world ought to be?

? *'Which of you, intending to build a tower, does not first sit down and estimate the cost, to see whether he has enough to complete it?' 'What king, going to wage war against another king, will not sit down first and consider whether he is able, with ten thousand, to oppose the one who comes against him with twenty thousand?' (Luke 14:28, 31)*

It sounds, Jesus, as if you are recommending forward planning. You seem to be saying, 'Look before you leap.' If I mismanage a project because I had not sat down beforehand to consider its effects, it is not enough for me to bleat, 'But I meant well.' You seem to want me to measure intentions against likely results. Is that your point? It seems so. Yet I cannot help feeling that you were not much into forward planning yourself. It does not seem like you. You said, 'Do not worry about tomorrow, for tomorrow will bring enough worries of its own. Today's trouble is enough for today.'

Maybe it is something else you have in mind – the cost of discipleship, the demand of commitment. You are a jealous lover, Jesus. You want all my love, not love rationed by the teaspoon. The measure of love is to be without measure, and you want to know if I am up to it. I have to answer in truth that I am not. I am in the category of 'Yes, but …' You are easy to please but hard to satisfy. You graciously accept even the smallest smidgen of goodwill but you never cease to ask for more.

You seem to answer your question just a little later when you say, 'So, therefore, none of you can become my disciple if you do not give up all your possessions.' You never do anything by half-measures, Jesus. Who can give up all their possessions? Do you mean us to be willing, if it comes to the crunch, to give them up, like martyrs giving up their lives? Or are you saying that the crunch is here and now, that the time for talking is over and for sharing has come? I say to myself that you do not need my house, car or money. But is that just a fudge? Plenty of people – and they are all your people, and therefore mine, too – need them. The world's resources are inequitably shared and I am part of that problem. I cannot do everything, but am I making that an excuse for doing nothing?

My greatest possession is myself, and I think that may be what you want. You want me. You want me to give myself to you unconditionally, saying, 'Not my will but yours be done.' You want my love, commitment, time and obedience. Maybe I need to start with the small things, to think globally and act locally, and work up from there. I do not want to be so heavenly as to be of no earthly use. I hope you will accept that, Jesus.

? *'If then you have not been faithful with the dishonest wealth, who*
• *will entrust you with true riches? And if you have not been faithful*
with what belongs to another, who will give you what is your own?'
(Luke 16:11, 12)

I do not find this easy, Jesus, but I think you are saying that if people
are not faithful with material wealth, such as money or property, it
is unlikely they will be faithful with spiritual wealth, such as truth-
fulness, integrity or honesty. 'What belongs to another' means
things that are external to us, while 'what is our own' means interior
wealth. I think you were saying the same thing in two different
ways.

It is facile for me to apply this to someone else and to point to
what they should or should not do. I have to think, Jesus, of how
this applies to me. Do I recognise that my ownership of property
brings social responsibility with it? Do I acknowledge that the
goods of the world are destined for the people of the world, that
every person has the right to find in the world what is necessary for
a human life, that sharing with others is a moral demand of my
humanity, not an optional extra to be exercised at my discretion?

Sometimes I fear that we are all worshippers of Mammon now.
We are driven by money; it preoccupies us from day to day, year to
year. For it we incur stress and more stress, seemingly believing
that it will all be worth it in the end. We sacrifice family life for it,
though we justify it in the name of the family.

Am I justified in keeping for myself what I do not need when
others lack necessities? Are they less human than I? Avarice is perhaps the most pervasive form of moral underdevelopment today.
The capitalist economic system seems to operate on the idea that the
sum of individual greed will constitute the public good – a senseless
superstition if ever there was one. The international imperialism of
money is triumphant and, like Moloch, devours children who go
hungry, empty their bodies of life fluids through chronic diarrhoea,
or are abandoned because parents have lost hope or died. Why?
Debt re-payment demands it.

I dare not ask, Jesus, what you are doing about this problem, because you might put the same question to me. If I am faithful in that
which is little, I will be faithful also in that which is great.

> **?** *Who among you would say to your slave who has just come in from*
> *ploughing or tending sheep in the field, 'Come here at once and take*
> *your place at the table'? (Luke 17:7-9)*

Who, indeed! Jesus, may I tell you a story? I think you like them.

In the days of the Habsburg Empire, it was the custom that when an emperor died he would be buried from the church of the Capuchin friars in Vienna, and traditional protocol was followed in the conduct of the funeral service.

As the cortège approached the church, the master of ceremonies of the imperial court would approach the locked door of the church, knock on it with his staff of office, and call out, 'Open the door to receive the body of his late majesty, Franz Josef von Habsburg' – or whoever it was. And he would list the titles of the dead monarch, who, since he had been an emperor, had many: he was not only Emperor of Austria but also King of Hungary, Prince of This, and Duke of That, Count of Somewhere Else and Knight Commander of many Orders. It made an impressive list of titles and honours. But the door would remain shut.

The master of ceremonies would knock again, 'Open the door to receive the body of the late Franz Josef von Habsburg.' This time there was no list of titles. Once again the door would remain shut.

A third time the master of ceremonies would knock on the door, this time gently with his knuckles, saying, 'I ask you to open the door to a poor sinner who asks for Christian burial.' And a voice from within would answer, 'Welcome, Christian!' and the door would open, the body be received into the church, and the Requiem Mass begin.

'Sceptre and crown come tumbling down,
  and in the dust be equal made,
  with the poor crooked scythe and the spade', wrote the poet.
Maybe the person who took you most to heart in this matter, Jesus, after Francis of Assisi, was not a Christian but a Hindu, Mahatma Gandhi … and he did it with such freedom. Asked why he travelled third class on the train, he replied, 'Because there is no fourth class.' To be unconcerned about status is an exercise of freedom.

? *'Were not ten made clean? But, the other nine, where are they? Was
none of them found to return and give praise to God except this for-
eigner?' (Luke 17:17-18)*

Ten lepers met you near a village on the road to Jerusalem, Jesus.
They were nine Jews and one Samaritan, an unlikely mix, divided
by race and religion, the Samaritan an outsider. They were united
only by misery. As the law required, they kept their distance, but
called out, saying, 'Jesus, Master, have mercy on us!'

They suffered from leprosy, a skin disease. But their problems
were more than skin deep. They were outcasts, cut off from society
by its ignorance, prejudice and fear. You told them to show themselves to the priests and, as they went, they were healed. One only
of them, and he the Samaritan, came back and gave thanks. It is not
surprising that you asked where the other nine were. It was those
'on the inside', so to speak, who took you for granted, while it was
the Samaritan, the outsider, who returned and gave praise to God.
A prophet is not without honour except in his own country and
among his own people.

One obvious point you are making, Jesus, is about gratitude. But
there is another as well: it is about being aware of what you do in us
below the surface, our becoming aware of what is happening within
us and around us. The more faithfully we listen to the voice within,
the better we will hear what is without. Were the nine ignorant or
simply bad-mannered? Were they just unthinking? Was their self-
absorption so total that it did not occur to them to look beyond
themselves, to pause, even for a moment, to say thanks to their heal-
er? They were aware of the change without, in their skin, but were
they unaware of the change within that you sought, in their soul?

You change the pattern of relationships. The outcasts become
again members of the community. The chosen ones make themselves strangers to you, the stranger becomes the chosen one, the
only one to whom you addressed the words, 'Your faith has saved
you.' Blessed are they who know their need of you.

I cannot help being struck yet again, Jesus, that here also, as so
many times elsewhere, you call us to awareness, to waking up and
being aware of what is happening. We daydream our way through
life. But you want us to be alive. Are we afraid of the freedom this
entails? Do we chose to be numb?

? *'Will not God grant justice to his chosen ones who cry to him day and night? Will he delay long in helping them? I tell you, he will quickly grant justice to them. And yet, when the Son of Man comes, will he find faith on earth?' (Luke 18:7-8)*

Your questions seem disconnected, Jesus. The first two are a pair, clearly linked. But the third seems to be on a different theme. Is that really so, or does it just seem so to me?

They come at the end of a parable about the need to pray always and not lose heart. You tell a story about a judge who neither feared God nor had respect for people. The two go together, don't they? As Dostoyevsky said, 'If God does not exist, everything is permitted.'

A widow came to him, looking for justice. You imply that she had right on her side. The judge was indifferent to her case, maybe because, as a widow, she would have no bribe to offer. But she persisted in coming, so, in the end, he consented to hear her case in order to be rid of her: 'She may wear me out by continually coming.'

If an unjust judge can be persuaded through sheer persistence to do justice, will not God, who is just, grant justice to his chosen ones who cry to him day and night? That is your question. The answer is obvious: yes.

You go on to say, 'I tell you, he will quickly grant justice to them.' Forgive me, Jesus, but I have to say that it does not always, or even often, look like that. I live in a country where a multitude of injustices of every kind has been swept under the carpet for decades. There they grew mouldy and stank. Now they are being brought into the open, and some justice is being done, in our imperfect human way. I am glad of that.

But it has been a hard, uphill struggle for injured people who must, at times, have despaired that their case would ever be heard. They were sometimes fobbed off with lies, sometimes belittled, or even ostracised as slanderers. Now at last they are gaining recognition and their case is being heard. That is progress, but how could it ever be called quick? Lawyers say, 'Justice delayed is justice denied.' Human justice is slow; I understand that, even if it is hard to accept.

But where was your hand, Lord, in quickly granting justice to your chosen ones who cried to you day and night? It seems absent. I can only say, 'I do not know.' But I believe that you can bring good out of any evil, and I trust you to do that.

? *'Who is the greater, the one who is at table or the one who serves? Is*
• *it not the one at table?' (Luke 22:27)*

It is indeed, Jesus. I enjoy sitting at a table where a meal is served,
and where someone else cleans up the mess and washes the dishes.
It is relaxing and enjoyable, conducive to conversation and convivi-
ality. But serving meals, with the preparation before and the clean-
up after, is a task that must easily lose its enjoyment and become a
chore.

Why is it that those who perform this service are among the least
well-paid, often dependent on tips and maybe eating the leftovers?
It is not so uncommon, too, for restaurant guests to amuse themselves by being patronising to waiters or waitresses, or making
jokes at their expense for the entertainment of their friends. Those at
table are indeed seen as the greater, but only because they have the
power of money, a power that lends itself to arrogance.

Your teaching, Jesus, was that power is a gift given for service,
not for domination – a teaching easy to understand but challenging
to live. You lived it yourself, you came among us as one who serves.
And the only real answer I can give you, the only answer to your
question that makes any difference, is not with words but with living.

I find it significant that you gave your teaching on service, and
then acted on it, washing the feet of your followers before institut-
ing the Eucharist, the supreme act of worship among them. Service
before worship; it reminds me of a story about your servant, Moses:
'As he was walking, Moses heard a shepherd praying to God, offering to serve him, to sweep his room, comb his hair, wash his clothes
and feet, bring him food, and kiss his hand. Moses scolded the shepherd for his blasphemy, "God does not need such services from
you!" The shepherd tore his clothes in despair and walked into the
desert.

That night God appeared to Moses and admonished him. "You
have separated my servant from me. I did not ordain worship for
my own benefit, but as a kindness to my servants. Their praise does
not glorify me, but bestows purity and radiance on them. I do not
look at their words, but at their spirit and emotions. I gaze into their
hearts to see if they are lovely, because the heart is the essence. I
want burning, burning! Light up your soul with the fire of love, and
burn all thoughts and words away!"' Thank you, Jesus. In your
Father's house, there are many rooms.

? *'Judas, is it with a kiss that you are betraying the Son of Man?'*
• *(Luke 22:48)*

Kissing was a normal part of men's greeting, nothing more than a peck on the cheek. But when you saw Judas coming to kiss you, Jesus, accompanied by an armed crowd, you knew that another agenda was present, so you asked him your question. It must have hurt you deeply to be betrayed by one you had chosen, one of your own, who had been with you, teaching, healing and helping.

When he came to kiss you, did you think of the proverb, 'From one who hates, kisses are ominous'? Many have been betrayed by a kiss, whether the mocking kiss of a two-timing lover, the ominous kiss of a Mafia godfather, the mercenary kiss of a prostitute, or the honey-trap kiss-and-tell of a mistress who has a contract with the tabloids.

I have a feeling that Judas's betrayal was different, that he did not sell you out for thirty pieces of silver, the official price of a slave in your time, simply because he was a money-grabber. Was he instead a man in the grip of an ideology, someone of fixed ideas who would not be dissuaded from the pursuit of a goal? Was he an ascetic who, once his head locked on an idea, shut down his heart and his humanity?

Ascetics are capable of self-sacrifice, determination and commitment – but also of ruthlessness. They would sacrifice someone for a principle, they live out of their head, and they are driven – not led – by ideas which are coherent, but narrow and rigid. Some Nazis, Afrikaners and Communists come to mind, such as Pol Pot of the Khmer Rouge patiently explaining to a journalist why it was necessary to kill children for the sake of the New Society, or Stalin remarking that while one death was a tragedy, a million deaths was merely a statistic. Ascetics may feel contempt for those less determined than they. They regard them as weak, contemptible, mere pleasure-seekers, without the diamond-hard edge to cut through obstacles in pursuit of a goal.

Was Judas that kind of man? Did he see you as one who had the qualities to drive out the Romans and become the king of a renewed, free Israel, but who refused to do so because of a prior loyalty to some – in his view – ethereal and insubstantial kingdom of God? Did he see you as squandering the best chance of freedom his people had had for generations? Was it in anger that he betrayed you?

Am I re-making Judas in my own image? Seeing others as I see myself?

? *'What are you discussing with each other while you walk along?'*
• *(Luke 24:17)*

Sometimes the obvious is that which is most easily missed. The truth which is staring me in the face is the one I am slowest to see and acknowledge. But if something looks like the truth, it is probably because it *is* the truth.

The two disciples on the road to Emmaus had been talking about the big news of the week, about you, Lord. You were a man of whom they had held great expectations; they had hoped you would be the one to set Israel free. Yet you had been killed by your own, the very people who should have been the first to recognise and welcome you. Your sad and cruel end had come as a bitter disappointment. The whole of Jerusalem had talked of nothing else. Yet here was this man alongside them who, seemingly, knew nothing about it.

The man beside them was you, Lord, in risen form, the very man they had been discussing. They had known you and been talking about you, but failed to recognise you when you walked with them.

That feels like a parable about myself, Lord. I know about you without knowing you. I walk beside you but do not recognise you. I am with you but do not meet you. I talk to you but do not listen to you. I have knowledge of you but do not acknowledge you.

Yet can it be otherwise, Lord? To ordinary people I relate by knowledge or experience, to you by faith – and that is of a different order. I am sometimes made to feel guilty by people who speak about an experience they have had of you as if they had met you like meeting a family member at home – directly, personally, intimately. I have never had that experience. Am I wrong to say that I do not expect to either, on this side of the grave? Does that mean that I am weak in faith, a half-baked, uncommitted Christian? I hope not.

We live and walk by faith, and faith is not sight. You give us glimpses of yourself, Lord, no more. If you gave us more, it might mislead us: we might adore the symbol instead of that which it symbolises. We might be satisfied with the glimpse, and not hunger and thirst for more. But the truth is that we are pilgrims and strangers here on earth, and our homeland is in heaven. Here we see as in a mirror, not your reality, face to face. There we shall become like you, because we shall see you as you really are. I am content with that.

? *'Was it not necessary that the Messiah should suffer these things and then enter into his glory?' (Luke 24:26)*

You asked this question, Lord, of two of your disciples as they walked to Emmaus in the days after your death. They had hoped that you would be the one to redeem Israel; they spoke of you as a prophet mighty in word and deed before God and all the people. Your death on the cross seemed an ignomious end to their hopes. A suffering Messiah was not part of their understanding.

Your question suggests that your suffering was necessary. I know suffering is an inescapable part of the human condition, but in what way was your suffering necessary? I think it was necessary for us as evidence of your love. Your solidarity with us in suffering gives our suffering meaning; you make it redemptive; you teach us how to cope with it, more indeed than merely cope, but how to make it growth-giving. You show us that if we wish to experience joy, we must be open to the possibility of suffering.

Your attitude towards suffering was full of paradox: you taught us to prevent, to relieve, and to accept it – all three. And each has value. I hope we never come to the point where we are so afraid of suffering, or repelled by it, that we remove from life anyone who reminds us of it, and think that we are being compassionate in doing so. Or have we reached that point already?

Suffering is a kind of visit from God that helps us to join love to knowledge so that both may be deepened. Our experience of suffering gives us a deeper level of solidarity with others. It safeguards us from superficiality, from hiding behind trivia, from a merely formalistic or functional religion. It clarifies vision and gives depth to love.

Of course, suffering need not lead to any of those things. It can break us, or it can make us tough, cold and cynical, afraid to hope lest we be thought naïve. It can harden us, so that we become incapable either of pain or joy. It can lead us to withdraw into a cocoon of self-pity. How it affects us is a choice that rests in our hands. I recall Dietrich Bonhoeffer writing about his fellow-prisoners in World War II that those were better able to endure suffering who had entered into the spirit of your passion.

You entered into our suffering, Lord, and you invite us to enter into yours. You were the suffering servant of God who accepted God's call, committed yourself to his service, bore witness to his truth, and died for others. You ask us to do the same. You say we should rejoice insofar as we share your sufferings, so that we also may be glad and shout for joy when your glory is revealed.

? *'Why are you frightened and why do doubts arise in your hearts?'*
• *(Luke 24:38)*

A favourite theme of yours, Lord. You came and stood among your close followers, men who had been with you for up to three years. You said to them, 'Peace be with you', but you nearly scared the life out of them. They had seen you die on the cross, and it must have been totally baffling to them that you now stood there, pointing to the wounds in your hands, feet and side.

I find it easy to understand their surprise. It takes me longer to understand their fear and doubt. Would it be right, Lord, to say that a basic problem, perhaps *the* basic problem, we have with the Christian faith is that it seems too good to be true? It teaches about God creating the universe in an act of gratuitous goodness, for no other reason than that the nature of love is to give. Love is creative. It speaks of God creating humanity in his image and likeness, endowing us with intelligence, free will, emotions, imagination and a body. It speaks of God intervening in human affairs, proposing, but not imposing, a better way than the one we choose. It tells us of God coming among us, not in power but in powerlessness, freely making himself so, for our sakes, so that by becoming like us we might become like him.

The story of your life, death and resurrection, Lord, does indeed seem too good to be true, the story of God becoming human so that we humans might – in a sense – become God.

We live in a world that is often cynical, quick with a jibe and a sneer, ready to belittle. And we sometimes flaunt our cynicism, calling it realism, though it is a voice of despair.

With that frame of mind, the story of your life seems like a dream – a beautiful one, indeed – but a dream all the same. Do we reject you and what you stand for, Lord, not essentially because it is too demanding, but because it seems too good to be true, because we are afraid to dare, to believe, to hope?

Is there not something in us that says to ourselves, 'You are not good enough for God. Do you think for one minute that God could possibly be interested in the likes of you? Don't fool yourself.' In the imagined superiority of our cynicism, that is to say, our pride, we belittle ourselves. You came to lift us up, to make all things new, to let us live life to the full.

? *'Have you anything here to eat?' (Luke 24:41)*

You had a down-to-earth sense of the practical, Lord. When you raised a young girl to life, you told her parents to give her something to eat. And you enjoyed meals, the company and conversation, I imagine, as much as the food and drink. You were not a vegetarian, nor did you abstain from alcohol; you had no time for the idea of 'forbidden' foods. You were not an ascetic, as we usually understand that term, with a lean and hungry look – and a temper to match. You allowed a woman to anoint your head with expensive ointment, you were happy in people's company, you enjoyed teasing your friends gently, you played with words, you spoke in images drawn from the day-to-day experiences of ordinary life.

In putting your question, Lord, you were making the point that you were neither a ghost, nor a memory, nor a projection, nor wish-fulfilment, but a man. And you made your point, as you so often did, with an action, a gesture, a fact – they cannot be argued away. You asked them for food, they gave it to you – a piece of broiled fish – and you ate it in their presence. Ghosts, memories, projections and wishes do not eat fish; humans do.

You asked them for food; they had not offered it. You took the initiative; they responded. They were probably day-dreaming, as they so often were – and we also – and it did not occur to them to make the offer. You gently woke them up.

Sometimes our image of you, Lord, is so heavenly as to be beyond our reach. We draw a mental picture of you as someone different from ourselves. We feel that you should be different from us, because we are not good enough to be like you.

Is that because we want to keep you at a safe distance, so as not to have to meet your gaze, respond to your questions, or enter into a relationship with you? Sometimes we prefer a functional religion of rituals and rules, where everything is cut and dried, where we do as we are told and do not ask questions. But you want to lead us beyond that, since that was the kind of religion the Pharisees had. And we are always returning to it, despite reminders like the Reformation that give us a fresh wake-up call.

Lord, you gave me eyes to see and ears to hear; you gave me a mind to think with, a memory to learn from, an imagination to dream with; you gave me a heart for feeling. Give me also, I ask you, the good sense to use them.

? *'What are you looking for?' (John 1:38)*

You put your question, Jesus, to two of the disciples of John. They answered, 'Rabbi, where are you staying?' They answered a question with a question, but I assume it contained the answer to yours. They wanted to know where you lived. You said, 'Come and see.'

The question is a basic one; it touches on the fundamentals. What am I looking for in life? I answer, 'Happiness.' But I know that I will never find happiness by directly looking for it. It comes only as a side-effect, a spin-off, when I look for something, or someone, else, outside of myself. You truly said, 'Those who find their life will lose it, and those who lose their life for my sake will find it.' If I ignore the clamour of self-will, then I find myself.

But maybe your question goes further than that. There are lots of people telling me what I should look for, what I should want or what they think I need. They are usually trying to sell me something that I neither look for, want, nor need.

I have to ask myself, 'What am I looking for?' Do I know? Maybe in all my rushing around I have not stopped to ask myself such a basic, obvious question. What do I actually want to do with my life? What am I looking for in it? Sometimes I spend my time running away, afraid to look at myself in truth and to come to know myself as I am. How can I know what I am looking for until I first know myself? That venture into the interior is the most challenging and daunting journey I can make, the forty centimetres from the head to the heart.

You said, 'Where your treasure is, there your heart will be also.' You urge me to look at myself, at my priorities, at the difference between wants and needs, at knowing what it is that I need. Maybe I will spend a lot of time in heaven thanking you for those prayers of mine on earth to which you gave the answer 'no', because I did not know what I needed.

If I find the key to my heart, I think that will be the key that opens to me the kingdom of heaven. Without the distortions of fear, may I know myself, Jesus, so that I may know you and, knowing you, may I love you as I love myself. To know, to accept, and to love myself as the stepping-stones to knowing, accepting and loving you – give me that, Jesus, in the small daily measures that I am capable of taking.

? *'Woman, what concern is that to you and to me? My hour has not yet come.' (John 2:4)*

Jesus, at the beginning of your public life, you were at the wedding feast in Cana when your mother noticed that your hosts had run out of wine. She pointed this out to you, without asking anything. It was a gentle hint, as if to say, 'They will be very embarrassed if they have to tell the guests that the wine is finished; do something about it.'

You spoke to your mother, addressing her as 'Woman'. This was a normal form of address by a man to a woman but not normal for a son to his mother. Scripture scholars assure us that it was not a rebuke. They point out that, on the cross, you addressed her as 'Mother'. I wonder. If something looks like an apple pie, and smells and tastes like one, it probably *is* one. If something sounds like a rebuke, it probably is one. The tone of the delivery counts, of course, and that cannot be conveyed in writing. Jesus, I think you did not want anyone, however close or well-meaning, to divert you from your priority: doing your Father's will. You wanted to make the statement that ties of flesh and blood were subordinate to your concern for his will. Having made that point, you then did as your mother wished. Mary of the Magnificat would have understood, and agreed.

Your relatives did not understand you, Jesus. That comes through clearly in the gospel. Its writers say that your parents did not understand what you said to them. And, later on, your relatives wanted to restrain you because people were saying that you were out of your mind. Was there perhaps not an element of irony drawn from personal experience when you said, 'One's foes shall be members of one's own household'?

God's ways are not our ways, Jesus, though we sometimes think we know better. We want to tame and domesticate God; I remember the person who said to me primly, 'I give the Lord his place.' You want us to transcend bonds that limit us and be ready to give ourselves to God unconditionally. The nearer I come to you, the nearer I will be to my relatives. The better I know you, the better I will know them. And if I wish to love them fully, may I first love you more than them. Then my love for them will be tested and true. If I put family or friends before you, I will end up far from you and, in the end, hate and blame them. You said, 'Strive first for the kingdom of God and his righteousness, and all these things will be given to you as well'.

? *'Are you a teacher of Israel, and yet you do not understand these things?' (John 3:10)*

You put your question, Jesus, to Nicodemus, who was one of the Sanhedrin, the supreme council of the Jews. You had a right to expect that he would be well versed in the teaching and traditions of your people. You spoke to him of a person being born again; he asked whether a person can enter for the second time into the mother's womb. He seemed to take your words in a crudely literalistic sense – or was he being sarcastic? And when you said, 'The spirit blows where it chooses, and you hear the sound of it, but you do not know where it comes from or where it goes,' he replied by asking, 'How can these things be?' Once more he seemed to miss your point. No wonder you exclaimed with surprise at the failure of a teacher to see and understand.

Was it that the mind of Nicodemus was locked into a system and unable to rise above it? The Pharisees – he was one – were great people for systematising. When that happens, theology is reduced to ideology. That the Spirit of God could blow where it chose, could come and go as it willed, was that an idea too universalist, too open to the interpretation that all people could receive the gifts of God in whatever way God chose to give them? Did this seem to Nicodemus to break dangerously through established boundaries, threatening the special status of the chosen people? How often does such narrowness, such closed adhesion to custom and culture, to tribe and tradition, to creed, code and cult present itself as loyalty, even while it divides people into we, the chosen, and they, the frozen!

Nicodemus was a sincere, courteous, cautious academic. By temperament he was probably unaccustomed to expect, or indeed to want, radical change. But you shook his scholarly assumptions. You challenged him to recognise that there before him you represented a breakthrough on a cosmic scale to a new order of reality. He could not see it, and remained in the darkness in which he came.

I have no right to be patronising or condescending about Nicodemus, since, just as much as he, I walk through life blindfold. If I do so, I do it by choice. No one did it to me, no one keeps it that way, but myself. You spoke about people preferring darkness to light. You spoke of those who do what is true – I like the word do – coming to the light.

I fear change; and that fear, more than selfishness, laziness or stupidity – all of which are also present in me – is what pushes me into a reactive, timid, unimaginative response to its challenge. Free me from my fears, Jesus.

98

? *'If I have told you about earthly things and you do not believe, how can you believe if I tell you about heavenly things?' (John 3:12)*

We find it difficult, Jesus, to look at old realities in a new way, or to recognise that change is taking place whether we wish it or not. We find change hard to accept, even when it is a change for the better. We dig in our heels and resist. You were trying to lead Nicodemus forward out of his fixed positions. He looked back to tradition and authority. He probably quoted texts and precedents. He may have pointed out the risks involved in change. His caution overcame his courage, his steadiness stifled his imagination.

Our resistance to change is partly a matter simply of not seeing what is happening around and within us. We take things for granted and discount them from our thinking because of their very familiarity, and despite their evident necessity. We nurture trivia while neglecting essentials. You asked how we can come to believe in the heavenly realities you pointed out to us, when we did not believe even the obvious earthly ones. In effect, you asked, 'If you miss the simple, how will you see the subtle?' Our blindness is a mystery. Why is it that having eyes we do not see, having ears we do not hear?

But the inner core of our resistance to seeing what is before us lies more in the will than in the intellect. It is a refusal, more than it is a failure, to see. 'There are none so blind…' Facing new realities often brings insecurity, a break from a peer group, a shaking of the foundations, a challenge to prevailing currents and trends. It may mean becoming politically incorrect. Why is it, too, that at times we are determined to live below our best, why do we belittle ourselves, why do we embrace mediocrity and shun excellence?

Why was it, Jesus, that you taught in parables? I think it was because you wanted to engage us, to draw us into a process of discovery by referring us to events or incidents that were commonplace in everyday life. And yet how often people failed to understand them, sometimes even after you had explained them. Was it the sense of urgency that characterised so many of the parables? Was it that people did not share your urgency, your sense that a unique moment in human history had arrived? Was it that the parables represented a call to decisive action when people felt more like cruising along in the familiar routine?

You said of yourself that you were the light of the world. Forgive me for choosing the darkness instead, for not wanting to see reality, which is the face of your truth.

? *'Do you want to be made well?' (John 5:6)*

Jesus, you asked the paralysed man a question, a simple, direct, plain, even obvious, possibly superfluous, question. He did not answer it. His reply was a complaint – or was it an excuse? He said, 'Sir, I have no one to put me into the pool … while I am making my way, someone else steps down ahead of me.' In effect, his answer was, 'It's not my fault that I don't get better; others are to blame.'

Perhaps, Jesus, your question meant, 'Do you want to let go the role of victim, or do you want to carry it with you always?' The man had been ill for thirty-eight years; surely in that time he could have found some way of getting into the healing pool. Had he succumbed to self-pity, demanding to be helped but refusing to accept it, except on his own terms? Was a state of helplessness a line of least resistance for which he had settled? Was he a passive personality, waiting for things to happen but not trying to make them happen, quick with excuses but slow with remedies? Had he the personality of the clinging vine, drawing life from those around, but not standing up to take responsibility for itself? Was he afraid of the demands that recovery would make of him?

Why did he not answer your question? Did he have what has been called 'the yokel blend of drowsiness and cunning'? All he had to do was say 'yes'; was that so difficult? Or did he not know his own mind? You wanted to know a person's real needs; it was to those you responded, not to the first idea that came from the top of a person's head. Maybe you asked him your question so that he might ask himself, perhaps for the first time, what he really wanted. Did he know what he wanted? Perhaps not; we don't always.

Your question makes the point that you looked for some co-operation from seekers; you did not do for people what they could do for themselves. You would not indulge either passivity or the mentality which sought to treat you as a magician who could work wonders regardless of human response.

Jesus, you ask me, 'Do you want to be made well?' I answer 'yes'. I want to be made well when I am paralysed by fear, by resistance to conversion or change, by the dead hand of routine, by mental stagnation, by emotional rigidity, by a sense of guilt that cripples, by lack of imagination, by anything that holds me back from living life to the full as you willed it. I do not want to be frozen or hardened, catatonic in selfishness. I want to hear your voice say to me strongly, 'Stand up, take your mat and walk,' or, in your words to the other paralytic, 'I order you: get up, pick up your stretcher and go.'

? *'How can you believe when you accept glory from one another and*
do not seek the glory that comes from the one who alone is God?'
(John 5:44)

Your question reminds me of something, Jesus. Towards the end of the 1990s, Robert McNamara, a former US Defence Secretary, wrote his autobiography. In it, he told of how he dealt with the principal problem of his tenure – the Vietnam war. He had studied the battle reports, the political assessments by embassy staff, the CIA briefings, and so forth. As a result, and over a period of years, he had come to the conclusion that the US could not win the war. Despite that, he continued to assure the incumbent president, Lyndon Johnson, that the US should continue to fight because the war could and should be won. He continued saying one thing while believing another. And so the war went on, with people on both sides continuing to die by the thousand.

As to why he did this, he explained that he knew that what he said was what the president wanted to hear, and it was expected of a person in his position to give that answer. He had to be seen to be strong.

I think, Jesus, you had something of that type of situation in mind when you asked your question about accepting glory from one another instead of from God. We do so. Careerism leads us to say what people in power want to hear, to give style priority over substance, to let the image of the office shape the reality of the office-holder rather than vice versa. The desire to climb up the greasy pole leads us to stand on the heads of those coming after, and lever ourselves up by pushing them down. It makes us strong with the weak and weak with the strong, a far from lovely human trait.

It happens in every kind of situation, because it is part of all our humanity. Sometimes we play politics with the truth, faithfully echoing the party line, the official orthodoxy, all in order to create the right impression among the right people. It is important to us to be respected, well thought of. Peer pressure is as powerful a force among adults as it is among teenagers, so we do not want to be seen as rocking the boat; we prefer to be a safe pair of hands.

Jesus, your precursor, John the Baptist, was described in his own time as 'A man wholly dedicated to the truth'. Fine words, but we look at what happened to him – he literally lost his head over it – and are afraid. And we look at you. You could have worked out a compromise with the Pharisees, the Sadducees, the high priests, the Roman procurator Pontius Pilate, you could have done a deal over a few bottles of wine. Instead, you chose to speak the truth whether anyone liked it or not. We know what it cost you, and we are afraid.

? *'Do you also wish to go away?' (John 6:67)*

You asked this question, Jesus, just after giving your disciples a teaching which many of them had found impossible to accept. You had spoken of yourself as the living bread that came down from heaven. You went on to say that those who eat your flesh and drink your blood have eternal life. That seemed beyond all reason to a people who could not accept, in the first place, that you had come down from heaven and, secondly, who interpreted your words in a materialistic sense that smacked of cannibalism. You asked them, 'What if you were to see the Son of Man ascending to where he was before?' You seemed to say that your ascension, which some of them would later witness, would bear testimony to your having come down from heaven. You reiterated your teaching by saying, 'The one who eats this bread will live forever.'

Because of that many of your disciples turned back and no longer went about with you. They said the teaching was difficult, and asked who could accept it. When they left, you then put your question to your twelve closest disciples.

Clearly, Jesus, you were not into the politics of consensus, religion as therapy, or teaching in sound bites; it was no part of your approach to ask what people might feel comfortable with; on the scales of your priorities the feel-good factor weighed less than a breath. One thing alone counted: truth.

You placed the highest premium on human freedom; you did not force anyone to say, do or choose anything. But, as part of that respect, you recognised that decisions produce effects, a yes or a no can have the greatest personal significance. I live in an age of capitulation which fudges issues rather than faces them, that softens the harsh edge of choice, that wishes to eat its cake and still have it. We all like to be on the winning side and we make the necessary adjustments.

You call on us to be committed, to drop the 'neutral' stance of agnosticism, to put our money where our mouth is. You want lovers, not detached inquirers, self-important posturers or cultured despisers. You want dedication, not unending postponement. You said that those who are not with you are against you. A person cannot, indeed, be neutral about you, because you are either the Son of God – as you said you were – or you were a demented megalomaniac, or the most unscrupulous conman that ever walked. You are either of supreme importance or of no importance at all.

Do I also wish to go away? No, Jesus, I wish to remain, to be committed, because I believe that you have the words of eternal life, that you are the Holy One of God.

? *'Did I not choose you, the twelve? And yet one of you is a devil.'*
• *(John 6:70)*

You were speaking, Jesus, of Judas, son of Simon Iscariot, for he, though one of the twelve, was going to betray you. You had chosen him along with the others. He had been your companion, eating bread with you on the way, an intimate sharing in your life. With the benefit of hindsight, the gospel writers – none of them as critical as John – call him a thief, saying that he used to steal what was put in the common purse. Here he is called a devil, a satan, literally, an adversary.

What did you see in him when you chose him? Did you suspect avarice? Did it occur to you that he might become a traitor? You were nothing if not observant and discerning, and I find it hard to believe you suspected nothing. Did you invite him anyway, accepting that life is limited, imperfect, ambiguous, paradoxical? Perhaps you were not trying to chose a perfect team but a representative group of humanity with its weaknesses and evil?

The end of your teaching on the Eucharist already looks ahead to the Last Supper. You spoke of your impending betrayal, saying that it would have been better for the one who betrayed you not to have been born. Your disciples were thrown into confusion by this, asking whom it could be. You gave a sign, without naming anyone, saying, 'The one who has dipped his hand into the bowl with me will betray me.' Judas asked, 'Surely not I, Rabbi?' and you replied, 'You have said so.' He immediately went out. And it was night.

I feel more sad than mad at this story of betrayal. I hate to see a good person stabbed in the back, to see trust meet with treachery, friendship with betrayal. You took Judas into your confidence, he was one of your inner circle, accompanied you on your journeys, heard you speak, saw your works of power, and then he literally sold you out. And for what? Thirty pieces of silver, the price of a slave.

I do not feel any better for knowing that Judas repented and brought back the silver to the chief priests and elders, saying, 'I have sinned by betraying innocent blood,' only to be met by a response of cynical indifference, 'What is that to us? See to it yourself.' Knowing that Judas then went on to meet a bad end, perhaps by suicide, I do not feel any sense of an imbalance corrected or justice served, but rather a bad situation made worse. Peter, after all, denied you three times but responded to it differently. He came to you, was forgiven, and went on to lead your followers. It is not the sins I commit that count so much as what I do about them afterwards. If I ever betray you, Jesus, may I follow the example, not of Judas, but of Peter.

?
• *'Did not Moses give you the law? Yet none of you keeps the law. Why are you looking for an opportunity to kill me? ... If a man receives circumcision on the sabbath in order that the law of Moses may not be broken, are you angry with me because I healed a man's whole body on the sabbath?' (John 7:19, 23)*

Am I right, Jesus, in detecting a note of anger in these questions? You were constantly trying to enlarge minds, while many people chose to keep theirs closed and to close also those of others. Determined small-mindedness is annoying, to say the least, especially when it parades itself as loyalty to tradition.

You were constantly challenged by people quoting the law of Moses at you. They knew all about what had been taught in the past and felt there was nothing to be said except by way of elaboration or commentary. You pointed out to them that, for all their professed allegiance to the law of Moses, they did not observe it. How, then, could they be so insistent on it in you? Jesus, you were an *à la carte* Jew, the very model of loyal dissent to your religious tradition; your ideas were *new* – a suspect word to official teachers. They had a universal character that went beyond the tribal, the sectarian or the merely ancestral.

I do not think that the gospel writers, inspired as they were by God, would have included so many of these controversies unless they had a significance which went beyond the circumstances of your time and place. If these were a matter of concern only to Jews, the gospel writers would have omitted them as merely local and transient. Yet these conflicts form a large part of the gospels, and the gospels were written for every age. They were written for us. Are you reminding me, Jesus, of the need to avoid replacing one religion of law with another one? Of the danger of changing the word made flesh back into mere words? Of reducing a living faith to a system of theology? Of trying to encapsulate the Spirit in an institution?

You came to set your people free from the intricacies and subtleties which leaders and teachers, in all good faith, had woven around the law and teaching of Moses. But people find security in the minutiae; they are afraid to let them go. And leaders' fear is that, if people are given an inch, they will take a mile. People are afraid to trust themselves because their leaders do not trust them.

The teachers were angry with you because you had healed a man on the sabbath, a day of rest from unnecessary activity. How closed and narrow their priorities were! And they saw such narrowness as fidelity. No wonder you called them blind guides leading the blind! May God forgive us.

104

? *'Woman, where are they? Has no one condemned you?' (John 8:10)*

You put your question to a woman caught in the act of adultery. She had been brought before you as a trap by the scribes and Pharisees. With an air of pretended innocence, they asked whether she should be stoned as the law of Moses prescribed. If you answered yes, you could be represented as cruel, and they could also denounce you to the Roman authorities who prohibited Jews from carrying out executions; if you answered no, they could say you were putting yourself above the law of Moses, which came from God.

You answered their question on your terms, not on theirs: 'Let anyone among you who is without sin be the first to throw a stone at her.' And they went away, one by one, beginning with the elders. Was it that the elders had a longer history of sin, or that they were smart enough to anticipate imminent defeat?

When they had gone, only two were left, misery and mercy. Then you put your question to the woman, and the answer was, 'No one, sir.' And you said, 'Neither do I condemn you. Go your way, and from now on do not sin again.'

The story raises questions:

Can a woman commit adultery by herself? Where was the man? Was there not a double standard among your questioners?

Were you trying to show that the way of blame and condemnation is not the way to bring the best out of people, that it usually drives them back defensively into themselves?

What was the significance of your writing on the ground? We have no mention of any other writing by you, and we do not know what you wrote. Did you do it to distract attention from the woman? Or was it to remind your watchers of the finger of God who wrote the commandments on Mount Sinai? God had said, 'Do not commit adultery,' but he did not add, 'and stone adulterers'. That was a human addition which claimed divine sanction. Thank you, Jesus, for extending forgiveness and the hope of freedom to one publicly humiliated, denied even the dignity of a name. You gave her a voice; you literally looked up to her while others looked down on her. You were compassionate also to her accusers: you did not demonise them; you tried to wake them up, to get them to look beyond the certainties they had identified with truth.

Jesus, today you are still writing on the ground with your finger: the power of God is creating new facts, bringing into being new events and realities at the grassroots. May I have eyes open to read them, and a heart open to their significance.

? *'Why do you not understand what I say? It is because you cannot accept my word.'* *(John 8:43)*

You answered your question, Jesus. But it still remains for me to answer. The obstacles that hold me back from following you are not intellectual, they are psychological. To put it in another way, they are in the will rather than in the mind. I make simple matters complicated so as to be able to keep postponing commitment, as if to say, 'When I get this sorted out, when I understand things clearly, then I will be able to give myself unreservedly. But how can I do that now with these unresolved issues?'

I rake up issues – anything from the Big Bang onwards will do – just so long as I can keep solemn and po-faced about them, not letting a sense of humour and proportion break through. I do this so as not to have to come out into the open and declare myself, so as not to have to face the challenge of personal change. I am like a man I spoke to who, when I asked him why he had kept God out of his life for so long, replied simply, 'It was easier to be an atheist.'

I make difficulties so that I can hold you at arm's length. They enable me to go on saying, 'Yes, of course, but ...' I make a difficulty about how the fact of pain can be reconcilable with the existence of an all-knowing, good and powerful God, but make no difficulty about the fact of pleasure, which you have associated with the simple things of life, like food, drink, sleep, sex and companions, even though it is not intrinsic to any of them. Why is pleasure a gratuitous gift? I do not know, but you will not hear me complaining. I have light enough to see, and darkness enough when I am so inclined.

I always want to hold back, at least a bit, though usually a lot, to hold on to some corner of my life as exclusively mine, where no one – not even you – may enter. But you are relentless, you claim all, you never settle for less than everything. I hold back, making intellectual fig-leaves to cover the nakedness of my fears, hoping that you will not see how foolish are the pretensions which I create to screen myself from you. But I do not think my bluff fools you; you have seen and heard it before.

I think, Jesus, that you were exasperated with the wilful, obstinate stubbornness of those who, like children in a tantrum, are determined to get their way, even if it hurts them. We adults sometimes have no more maturity than the child who will punish himself in frustration rather than accept that he was wrong, or smash a toy rather than share it. Help me not to take myself so seriously that I cannot stand back and laugh at my folly. Then I will have tamed it and begun to welcome the truth.

?
• *'Which of you convicts me of sin? If I tell the truth, why do you not believe me? (John 8:46)*

Why do we not believe you, Jesus? You spoke the truth, and the human mind is orientated towards truth; it is hungry for it. Our mind recognises it connaturally. And the truth proposes itself gently, in freedom; it imposes nothing, offering itself for our acceptance only because it is true.

Your experience, as described in the gospel, was one of almost constant resistance and opposition. Mostly that came from religious leaders and teachers.

Why? They seemed trapped in positions of their own making; they painted themselves into corners; they made absolutes out of what was relative; for every dilemma they had a formula, and for every transgression a sanction. Whether it was issues like the observance of the sabbath, the baptism of John, or attitudes towards Gentiles, they were locked into positions from which they could not extricate themselves. They fell back on trying to score cheap debating points, using truth as a tactic of convenience. Truth as truth did not seem to interest them. They looked at how it would play out politically, *vis-à-vis* Roman authority or the traditions of their own faith community. Their questions were: How will this work out? What are its implications? How will people react? Does this contradict what we said earlier?

It is hard to avoid the conclusion that they were mentally locked into considerations of power and control. Their priority was not to rock the boat, not to 'upset' people, not to go against traditional positions for fear of undermining their authority. That was not your way. They yielded to the temptations you rejected in the desert.

In that respect they were to be pitied. Their inflexibility belittled the mystery of God, which is always beyond our grasp. It was an evasion of the challenge to growth. It expressed fear of the dynamic character of truth. Their thought was to hold on protectively, to keep a firm grip on the reins, and they stifled the Spirit. They turned inwards on themselves, as if they held the copyright of truth. This suffocated their people, even while the external appearances were maintained to the full.

Jesus, liberate me from fear of the truth. May I be faithful to it, going wherever it leads. In you, truth was not an abstraction, not a dry, unemotional concordance with reality, to be reached by detached analytical objectivity. In you the truth was personal, warm flesh and blood, to be welcomed with an embrace.

? *'Do you believe in the Son of Man?' (John 9:35)*

Yes, Jesus, I do. I believe that you were a person, truly and genuinely, like the rest of humanity. I believe that, for love of us, you, the Son of God, became Son of Man, and did not refuse to descend to our human condition in all things, including ignorance, but excluding sin. Sin disfigures and diminishes our humanity. I do not become more human, but rather less so, by sinning. You could no more accept sin than love could accept hate.

As a child you grew in wisdom and knowledge. You did not go through life acting out a role, playing a part. When you asked a question, it was not in the manner of a teacher who asks merely to test the students. You asked because you did not know.

I think you applied the title Son of Man to yourself as a way of saying that you were a man of earth, living an earthly life, though destined for heaven. You had a powerful sense of your mission from your Father to proclaim the kingdom of God. For you there was one kingdom of God, not two, a heavenly and an earthly, one upstairs, the other downstairs. You said that the kingdom of God is among us, that is, in our relationships. It is about how we relate to each other.

You were the embodiment of God, God-among-us, not God across the sea or beyond the mountains, but God inseparable from us in our human struggles. You were emotional, not aloof and dispassionate, like the gods of the Greeks. You enjoyed meals, company and celebrations. You were loved by women and stood up for them. You felt sympathy for people in their difficulties. You touched and were touched by people. You struggled with fear, you felt tired, hungry and thirsty. You were down-to-earth and practical. You cried when your friend died. You earned your living from your work. You were jostled by crowds. You took a rest. You were impatient at lack of imagination. You felt like giving up. You loved children. You lost your temper with the money-changers in the temple. You were shrewd and perceptive. You loved your mother. You experienced depression. You prayed and received no answer; you felt forsaken by God. You were misunderstood by relatives, frustrated by the stupidity of your followers, angered by the deviousness of your critics, betrayed by friends, sold out by a disciple, unjustly condemned by those who should have welcomed you, and executed by a coward. Though sinless, you felt the weight of human sin. You surrendered to God with a faith unsupported by props.

Do I believe in such a Man? Yes, I do; in him I can recognise someone like myself. I feel a sense of kinship. You are not a stranger to me.

? *'I have shown you many good works from the Father. For which of*
• *these are you going to stone me?' (John 10:32)*

A moment before you asked your question, Jesus, the Jews had taken up stones to stone you. Your response was to keep pointing to your works as witness. In effect, you said, 'Look at what I do. Could the person who does such things not be in union with God? If that is the case, then why do you want to stone me?'

Throughout the gospels there is this incessant hostility towards you from the leaders of your people. If they could not fault your actions, they said you did them in the wrong way (such as on the Sabbath) or for the wrong reason (because you were possessed by Satan). This stubborn, unyielding refusal to acknowledge good as good is an example of the perverse tribute that evil pays to good. Evil twists whatever is good, misrepresents it, belittles it, sniggers at it – in short, does anything but acknowledge it for what it is.

But not everyone was like that; some were different. There were people who accepted you, Jesus, people who ignored the slippery games of *Catch Him If You Can*. They were those who experienced suffering. It does not surprise me at all that the cripples, the blind, the deaf, the outcasts, the disreputable, the guilty, indeed all those weighed down by the burdens and cares of life, were not to be found among those who sought to trap or to trick you.

Their suffering had stripped away from them all that was false, insincere or superficial. It had stripped them down to the essentials. If we are in pain we do not have either the disposition or the energy to play tricky games to see if we can trip up a person who might be able to help us. Suffering tears away the masks we hide behind; it breaks through the hardened crust of resistance and makes us stand before the world naked, as we really are. Desperation leaves no room either for flippancy or deviousness.

I think that suffering may give a heightened receptiveness to truth. It can clarify issues, reducing them to the essentials, undistracted by trivialities and irrelevancies. One of the lasting memories, Jesus, that I have from my time in Africa is of a suffering people. And yet it is not the suffering I remember so much as that nowhere else have I met people who were so able to keep hope alive in the face of apparently hopeless situations. Jesus, you do not conform to our human rules of how things should be; you do not operate according to our expectations. And thank you for that.

? *'Are there not twelve hours of daylight?' (John 11:9)*

You asked this question, Jesus, just after your disciples had warned you of the danger of going back to Judea where the Jews had just before tried to stone you. You went on to say, 'Those who walk during the day do not stumble, because they see the light of the world. But those who walk at night stumble, because the light is not in them.'

I know that light and darkness are a favourite theme of John who wrote this gospel, and he makes significant comments about morning and evening, night and day, light and darkness, at strategic moments in your story. This moves me to look for an allegorical meaning to your question, which I find difficult to understand.

You had earlier described yourself as 'the light of the world', so I take it that when you spoke of those who do not stumble, you meant those who walk in your light, who follow you, who commit themselves to you. By contrast, those who do otherwise are like those who walk at night and therefore stumble 'because the light is not in them'. You said, 'This is the judgment, that the light has come into the world, and people loved darkness rather than light because their deeds were evil.' Mysterious, but true.

I know, too, that in John's gospel the word 'Jews' is a kind of short-hand for those who close their minds and slam shut the door of their hearts. What strikes me, Jesus, about unbelievers I meet is that often they seem shallow, lacking in depth. They remind me of ice-skaters, skimming fast over the surface of things, but never really entering into anything. They are a world apart from the person who is truly searching, groping in the dark perhaps, who has not yet found you. I feel sorry for those who can be lightly dismissive of faith, as if they say, 'I have no need of that,' 'I've outgrown that infantile fixation,' or simply, 'I can't be bothered.' I can sense a hollowness in them, and it rings empty. The TV soaps come to mind.

In my lifetime I have met people of different religions and varying degrees of commitment. Their faces – we all have made our face by the time we are forty – look like they have been lived in. There is something going on inside them, something that is often difficult and challenging, but real. And they are alive. I feel sorry for those who miss out on that; there is a depth that is missing from them. I wonder if they ever stop, in a quiet moment, look themselves in the eye, and ask themselves when they are going to stop running, when they are going to bring the great game of evasion to an end.

'Are there not twelve hours of daylight?' You seem to say, 'Use them while they last.'

? *'Everyone who lives and believes in me will never die. Do you believe this?' (John 11:26)*

Jesus, when you first put that question to Martha, whose brother Lazarus had died four days previously, it must have been agonisingly difficult for her. Did she reason with herself, 'If I say no, will he refuse to help? If I say yes, am I telling lies?' The gospel account makes it sound as if she spoke with no shadow of doubt. But she can hardly have been so assured; the idea of resurrection from the dead was far from universally accepted. And, Jesus, what your question implied about yourself was staggering. It was not a challenge to be met by a facile answer.

Jesus, you brought Martha's hope, which related to the future, into the realm of the present. She used the word 'will'; you used the word 'am'. You had said to her, 'I am the resurrection.' It is in the present that the real test of faith comes. I can be brave about choices that relate to the future; it is those in the here-and-now that challenge me. And those are the ones that interest you. When I am young and healthy I can be brave about the prospect of death; but face to face with a death in the family, or the knowledge that the sands of time do not have far to run for me, the question assumes a different level of urgency.

Your question to me is, 'Do you believe this?' Yes, Jesus, I believe. I cannot accept that the human person, in whom you have planted the seeds of greatness, the hope of truth, justice, love and freedom in their perfection, will not attain those – and much more beyond my imagining, of which they are only an image. God does not play games with us, planting impossible hopes in our hearts; he does not make fools of us by raising our hopes only to dash them. God is not a mocker.

But, Jesus, I think there is another level of meaning. You are also saying that whoever receives the gift of life through faith in you will not die a spiritual death. That relates to life on earth, where the kingdom of heaven begins. Those to whom you give the gift of faith will find purpose and meaning in life. They will have a sense of values, a conscience to enable them to live and do the truth, a pattern of relationships that will give their life a focus, an integrated character, and motivation to energise them from within. Those are good gifts for life, and I am glad that you have given them to us. They are not of our making; they are given. That I believe.

? *'Did I not tell you that, if you believed, you would see the glory of*
• *God?' (John 11:40)*

Your question, Jesus, is a statement about yourself, one that no ordinary human being would dare make. It was a statement about your relationship to God your Father, about who you were, and what your mission was.

A moment before you had been greatly distressed. Why? Was it by the death of Lazarus? Hardly, since you thanked your Father for having heard your prayer to raise him. It seems more likely your distress was caused by the refusal to believe of those who stood there. They had said to each other that, if you could open the eyes of a blind man, then you should have been able to prevent Lazarus from dying. The image that comes to my mind is of people standing with arms folded across their chests, smugly solid in their complacent certitudes, waiting for another opportunity to belittle. Was there some peer pressure at work in them, an element of competition to see who could come up with the most cynical and debilitating wisecrack?

It seemed that every effort on your part to bring them to belief served only to precipitate a further withdrawal, every act of goodness met with yet more cynicism. Theirs was not a failure to believe but a refusal of belief; they lived on their vindictive pride, like a man dying of thirst in a desert, sucking blood from his own body to assuage his thirst. Never satisfied, refusing all offers of forgiveness, they could only be left to themselves – and that is what hell is, the choice of the self against the other.

I think of your words to the people about Lazarus: 'Unbind him, and let him go.' Like all your words and actions, Jesus, they had a wider audience than merely those who were then present. They are about me. I pray that I may never be bound by the frozen anger of cynicism but be angry, if there is good reason for it, with passion and fire. May I have a passion for truth and justice, a hatred for humbug and hypocrisy, a fire in my blood against fudge and deceit.

You said, 'If you believe, you will see the glory of God.' May I believe wholeheartedly, not by teaspoonfuls; may I commit myself unreservedly to focusing my life on God, not on self. In this, may I neither dither nor equivocate but be single-minded, like those of whom you said that they shall see God. 'If I believe' – I believe, Jesus; strengthen me in it.

? *'Now my soul is troubled. And what should I say – 'Father, save me from this hour'?' (John 12:27)*

There is a sense of foreboding about this question, Jesus, that things are moving to a climax, though not a climax in the sense of your work having come to completion. On the contrary, you were troubled by the constant presence of unbelief; it was relentless and inescapable. There was no sense that you were gradually winning the struggle, rather of the light being smothered by darkness. The carping and criticism of your enemies took on a sharper edge. There is a sense of their closing in for the kill, surer now of their ground. Increasingly you seemed alone, though you were not, for the Father was with you.

You knew what was in people, you knew what had happened to the prophets that had gone before you. With your perceptiveness you must have known what was coming, if not the how or the when of it. Not without reason, you were troubled by fear.

Beneath the fear there must also have been a quiet, hidden joy, an inner knowledge that fulfilment was near, that your mission was drawing to its culmination. That this would cost you pain, you could not have been in doubt. And yet, through all that, there was your assurance of being at one with God your Father.

You always called God 'Father', not a unique title among the Jews of your time, but unique in its pre-eminence in your life. You were so focused on your Father; everything began, continued and ended with him. He was central to you and, in all moments of decision or crisis, your attitude to him was, 'Not what I want, but what you want.' For you, your Father was all.

Were you going to ask your Father to save you from the suffering that was coming? But the suffering was the badge of love, the deepest sign of your commitment, and was inseparable from your mission. To have asked to be saved from it would have amounted to asking to be relieved of your mission. But it was for that reason that you had come to that hour, to that moment of decision. It was the time to plunge into the crisis, to make a final act of surrender, not knowing anything except that your Father would not abandon you.

You called on him to glorify his name, to proclaim his presence and power. And he answered, 'I have glorified it, and I will glorify it again.' Though you said that his voice was for the people's sake rather than for yours, it seemed to strengthen you to face the death that was coming. In my moments of fear and uncertainty, my anxiety about the future, may I follow your example of unswerving trust in God our common Father.

? *'Do you know what I have done to you? (John 13:12)*

Jesus, not for the first time, you are calling me to awareness. You are saying to me: 'Wake up and look at what is going on around you, and within you. Don't sleep-walk your way through life. Come alive and be aware.'

Do I know what are you doing in my life? – I think that is what your question means. You had just washed the feet of your followers, a task normally done by a slave. You did the work of one who would not even be noticed by others, much less receive a word of thanks. You placed service before Eucharist. Personal status and dignity meant nothing to you. Power, position, possessions – we see them as important. You say they are not, but instead that menial service of others is. You pose a different order of priorities, one that would never have occurred to me had you not lived and taught it.

You turn my values upside down, Jesus. I would have thought of God's action in terms of power. But you say that the only value of power is in service; and any other use is idolatrous. That is a quiet revolution. It goes against the grain with me because of my love of power. People respect – or is it fear? – the powerful, even when they abuse power. The pages of history would be short indeed if the story of the drive for power were removed.

You often said, 'Do not be afraid.' It is the commonest phrase in the Bible. We are afraid of what is within us, afraid of our potential for greatness, afraid of the possibility of success, so that we fail and fall like someone on a ledge who becomes dizzy and allows fear to take control. Yet you keep telling me not to be afraid, and that must cover all fears.

Your way of working in us, Jesus, is usually indirect. What you bring about in us is, more often than not, a side-effect, an unexpected spin-off from the predictable course of things. I think of people who prayed for a cure of an illness and did not receive it. Instead they received healing of something else, perhaps being enabled to let go of unforgiveness or anger that had held them bound in resentment and bitterness, or else being enabled to accept the illness with a good grace. They were not cured, but they were healed. I know people who were given a job they did not like, but they accepted it and gave it their best effort, only to find that they came to like it and, perhaps, in the process to discover talents and abilities they never knew they had.

Open the eyes of my soul, Jesus, to see what you do in me, for me, with me and through me. And may I give you thanks for it.

Jesus, you had just told Peter that he could not then follow you to death. He had answered, 'Why can I not follow you now? I will lay down my life for you.' In reply you asked your question, adding, 'Very truly, I tell you, before the cock crows, you will have denied me three times.' You gave him a sharp rebuke, Jesus. I cannot believe you did so because you enjoyed deflating his generous, if over-stated, goodwill. Peter's mouth ran ahead of his mind. He was full of well-meaning talk, but the gap between promise and fulfilment was long and large. That finds an echo in me.

When he was with you on the holy mountain, he had had an experience of God that went beyond the power of words to describe. His reaction was to want to capture it in a structure, saying, 'Let us make three dwellings, one for you, one for Moses and one for Elijah,' as if that way he could hold on to it. Luke, the gospel writer comments, 'He did not know what he was saying.'

When you spoke, Jesus, about your forthcoming suffering and death, it was Peter who took you aside and began to rebuke you, saying, 'God forbid it, Lord! This must never happen to you!' You turned to him, uttering the savage words, 'Get behind me, Satan! You are a stumbling block to me; for you are setting your mind, not on divine things, but on human things.' Once again he had misunderstood, unable to grasp that yours was the way of self-effacement, not self-assertiveness.

And in Gethsemane, it was Peter who took up the sword to defend you. I sometimes imagine that Peter was older than you, Jesus, thought you needed looking after and that he had a mission to do that – Peter, always and everywhere getting it wrong, always and everywhere mistaking the ways of power for those of service, wanting to control you, and thinking of it as love.

Just before you asked your question, Jesus, Peter had promised loyalty to you, saying, 'Even though all become deserters I will not. Even though I must die with you, I will not deny you.' And then he did just that, deny you, not once but three times.

Peter was a slow learner. Is it harsh to describe him as sincere but stupid? It probably is. It is easier for me and for the Christian community since we have the benefit of hindsight. But we still play the power game, still believe that God needs to be managed, that you need keeping an eye on, Jesus, in case your constant insistence on freedom gets out of hand. We have the spirit of the Grand Inquisitor among us. When will we learn to trust the Spirit of God present among us and stop trying to manage God?

? *'In my Father's house there are many dwelling places. If it were not*
• *so, would I have told you that I go and prepare a place for you?'*
(John 14:2)

You seem to be saying, Jesus, that there is plenty of room in heaven, your Father's house, not just 144,000 places; and there are no seats reserved for an elite, no gradations or degrees of access. If I may use human ideas and language (what else have I?) in speaking of heaven, I think there may be surprises at who is and who is not 'there'. But can God's will to save, his salvific purpose, ever ultimately be thwarted? Perhaps all will be there – in the end.

Neither will I need a Michelin guide, telling me that this particular part is worth a detour: 'What no eye has seen, nor ear heard, nor the human heart conceived, what God has prepared for those who love him – these things God has revealed to us.' It is beyond my imagination; indeed, if I could have a realistic idea of what heaven was like, it would not be worth having.

Heaven is being in the presence of God by mutual indwelling. We will abide in God and God in us. This indwelling, already begun on earth through faith and baptism, is brought to completion in heaven. Heaven is about a new pattern of relationships: 'The home of God is among mortals. He will dwell in them as their God; they will be his peoples, and God himself will be with them; he will wipe away every tear from their eyes. Death will be no more; mourning and crying and pain will be no more.'

Heaven is outside of time, which was created by God. With, or in, God, there is neither past nor future, only an eternal present. Is heaven also, in some sense, a continuation of the present? – if I have closed myself against God here, can I be open to God hereafter? If I have shut out people on earth, can I be open in heaven to God who created them?

Jesus, I believe you are not making fools of us, leading us on with the hope of a non-existent pie in the sky when we die. I believe you spoke the truth when you said that you have gone to prepare a place for us; and it is a gift, not an achievement.

In the final analysis, heaven is a mystery. All I know is what you have told me, that then we will be like you for we will see you as you are. And that is enough for me. May its vision and hope sustain me in my darkness.

? *'Have I been with you all this time, Philip, and you still do not know me? Whoever has seen me has seen the Father. How can you say, 'Show us the Father'? Do you not believe that I am in the Father and the Father is in me?' (John 14:9-10)*

Who are you, Jesus? That is the question that runs through much of the gospel. A moment before, Thomas had implicitly asked it. And now Philip, another disciple, is also asking it. I ask it; everyone asks it.

Your questions reveals impatience with Philip for his inability to grasp who you are. Your unity with your Father was at the heart of your life. You are in the Father and he is in you; the Father and you are one. It is as if you are saying, 'The truth is simple; why do you want to complicate it? I have come from the Father, live in the Father, and will return to the Father. In him I live and move and have my being. How much simpler can I make it?'

You know very well, Jesus, that floods of ink have been used in writing not just books, but whole libraries, in attempts to answer the question of your identity: How much did you know of yourself? How can a person be both divine and human? Can someone be divine and not know it? Were you truly yourself or a divine puppet? These controversies took up several centuries of the early life of the Christian community, and they had to be addressed if the Christian faith were not to be dismissed as inherently contradictory.

You were saying, I think, that you were present to the Father and he to you. You were united to him and yet distinct from him. You did not form a single unity, but were one in mind and heart, so to speak. You were the image of the invisible God, God made visible to us and tangible by us. You were the mediator, the bridge, the connecting link between the transcendence and the immanence of God. If we want to know what God is like, we look to you. In your person you say to us all we are capable of understanding about God, who is beyond our understanding. You, Jesus, the carpenter from Nazareth, were God's self-disclosure to us. You were, literally, the embodiment of God, God come among us as one like ourselves in a body like ours.

For me, Jesus, and I think for others also, the hard part is to accept your humanity, to grasp that you were truly human, not acting out a role, but truly coming to a knowledge of the unique relationship you had with your Father. I do not think that any intellectual concepts will ever take hold of that reality. May I have the spiritual intuition that it fits, it is congruent, that, in some deep way which is not irrational, though going beyond reason, it is coherent.

Your disciples had just said, 'We know that you know all things …
We believe that you came from God.' But your question, Jesus,
showed you felt they did not believe in you, despite what they had
just said.

What is it to believe? I think the Latin word, *credo*, which means
I believe, gives a clue. *Credo* comes from two words, *cor*, meaning
heart, and *reddo*, meaning I restore. Through frequent use *cor reddo*
became *credo*. And *credo* means I restore my heart. The Latin word
includes intellectual assent but goes beyond it. It involves the heart,
affection, emotion, love. It is a commitment of one person in their
totality to another. It means the heart is restored to where it belongs.
There is, to borrow a phrase, a God-shaped gap in human con-
sciousness, where God had always been. To believe is to fill that gap
with the only reality that can fill it – God.

The disciples thought in all sincerity that they did believe but,
Jesus, you knew them better. You knew that they would soon be
scattered, each one of them, leaving you alone. They loved you, but
their love had not been tested in the fire of persecution.

You knew that persecution was coming, so you urged them to
take courage. In this instance you seemed to see their lack of it as the
obstacle to their belief. They could not commit themselves to you
while simultaneously looking over their shoulder to see if the
wolves were coming.

That rings a bell with me. In our time political correctness is a
hidden censor, intimidating people, terrifying them of being found
on the wrong side of conventional wisdom. People are afraid of the
ostracism that may follow from flouting the unwritten rules. Peer
pressure produces conformism in the trends we follow, not only in
drinking and dress but, more importantly, in ideas and attitudes.
Such lack of moral courage is not a pleasant sight and few mistake it
for genuinely free thought. Simple examples are where vulgarity is
defended as honesty, or shameless behaviour as sincerity, which is
just what it is not. It is more significant and influential at the level of
ideas: how difficult, almost impossible, it has become to discuss issues of race for fear of being accused of racism. That hinders efforts
to face problems of under-development in the Third World in a
helpful or effective way. Such moral cowardice is found in any and
every sector of society.

I admire courage, Jesus, but I am as much of a coward as anyone. Help me.

? *'Whom are you looking for?' (John 18:4, 7)*

Jesus, there are only two questions that you asked three times in the New Testament, and this is one of them. It must have been important. Twice you asked it of Judas and his supporters when they were about to take you prisoner, and then you asked Mary Magdalene after you had risen.

What do you mean by the question? I am looking for *you*. Who else?

Do you mean, 'What kind of God am I looking for?' Is it the bearded old man up in the sky, so beloved of cartoonists? No, I let that idea go along with the other bearded old man up in the sky, the one with a bagful of presents over his shoulder who comes down the chimney at Christmas – though it took me much longer to do it.

Am I looking for God the fire brigade – sent for in emergencies and ignored the rest of the time? Or is it God the insurance policy: I feel it is better to be on the safe side, I never know when I might need him. He does not ask for much but the penalty for ignoring him if he is there could be great, so why not go along? You pay the dues and you get the benefits. Or is it the long-distance God: the kindly, ineffectual, but remote figure who really does not make much difference, but whom it is better to humour, just in case? Or is it God the moral censor, the God who never misses anything, who knows my unspoken thoughts, innermost secrets, the recording angel at his side, noting my sins? Or is it God the super magician who can pull rabbits out of the hat at the last minute when all else fails?

What kind of God am I looking for? Your questions are difficult, Lord, and I do not know how to answer them. I do know what kind of God I am not looking for. I do not want a God who is a product of my own mind, the conclusion to a syllogism, the end product of a 'proof'. Neither do I want a God who is a bigger and better version of myself, one made in my image and likeness. That God I can never adore.

I want to unload from my mind all my ideas and images of God because they are certainly inadequate, probably inaccurate, and likely misleading. They are idols and I do not want to be an idolater.

I will wait, Jesus, wait in reverence and silence. God is. I do not know *what* God is, I believe *that* God is – and that is enough for me. 'When he is revealed, we will be like him, for we will see him as he is.' That is enough to keep me going. Thank you, Jesus.

? *'Am I not to drink the cup that the Father has given me?' (John 18:11)*

This is like the question you had put to your disciples, Jesus. You had asked them, 'Are you able to drink the cup that I must drink?' Drinking the cup meant entering into the suffering fully, draining it to the last drop. Your question was rhetorical; its answer was obvious. You would not shirk from drinking the cup nor look for an easy way out. You were drunk, Jesus, but not from wine: there was one central preoccupation which intoxicated you, and that was to do your Father's will. Nothing else mattered.

Nor did you ask your followers to do anything you yourself were not prepared to do. You were faithful to your own precept about doing and teaching.

Jesus, why did you have to die? Why did suffering have to be so much a part of your work of salvation? In what sense – how – did you take on yourself the sins of humanity and wipe out our guilt by your death? Does that not remove from us our responsibility for ourselves? Were you a scapegoat on a cosmic scale? Did your death give your Father satisfaction, as some of the saints have taught? Could it all not have been otherwise? Does it not lead your followers to an unhealthy pre-occupation with suffering? I remember a person say to me, 'We are put here [on earth] to suffer.' Does that not feed a passive, fatalistic acceptance of suffering as sent by God, the idea that whatever happens is God's will because, if it wasn't, it would not have happened? In Catholic churches an image of you as crucified is given a prominent place; does that not have the effect of setting your resurrection to one side, and giving primacy to just one part of the process of our salvation, and that not its completion but an intermediate stage?

These are just some of my questions, Jesus. I ask them as I struggle to understand yours. I know the 'official' answers to my questions; they do not satisfy me. Maybe I should not expect them to. Perhaps it is better simply to say, 'I do not know', and leave it at that.

But I know that there is a link between love and suffering, a link which goes beyond logic, reason and practicality. Suffering represents a call to solidarity. By your suffering you associated yourself with every person who suffers. Your suffering redeems human suffering and makes it redemptive. You show me a life lived sacrifically, lived for others. You said your food was to do the will of him who sent you and to complete his work. Jesus, I cannot claim to understand; indeed I know I do not. Maybe that does not matter: 'The heart has reasons of which reason knows nothing.'

? *'If I have spoken wrongly, testify to the wrong. But if I have spoken*
• *rightly, why do you strike me?' (John 18:23)*

When you were questioned by the high priest, Jesus, about your disciples and your teaching, you answered that you had always spoken openly to the world, you had said nothing in secret, so the priest should ask those who heard what you had said and they would give evidence. When you said that, one of the police standing nearby struck you on the face, saying, 'Is that how you answer the high priest?'

This slap, a deliberate public humiliation, was given by a sycophant, a self-appointed defender of authority, trying to win favour with those in power. I know the type, more Roman than a pope, more royal than a queen – but ready to do a U-turn should the scales tip the other way. What he did was illegal in a Jewish court. But enough about him.

You answered, 'If I have spoken wrongly, testify to the wrong. But if I have spoken rightly, why do you strike me?' That is an unanswerable argument, but only when coming from someone who is innocent. It shows me that you were not a passive figure, taking an attack lying down; you defended yourself.

But you did not hit back when he struck you. You had taught, 'If anyone strikes you on the right cheek, turn the other also.' You practised what you preached. That breaks the spiral of violence, the cycle of attack responded to by counter-attack, aggression evoking reprisal. It helps to create a new pattern of relationships in which evil does not have the last word.

I know, Jesus, that it is forgiveness, not revenge, which is cathartic, which gives release from anger. I remember Nikita Khrushchev, the former leader of the Soviet Union, saying that if someone hit him on the cheek, he would not turn the other one; he would hit back so hard he would break the other person's jaw. I have sometimes felt the same, hearing in my heart the voice that says, 'Don't get mad, get even.'

But I have learned this much: vengeance multiplies evil; it is justice that redeems it. I know that as long as I refuse to forgive, I am bound by the evil the other has done to me; I become like those I hate. I know, too, that if I forgive, I – not the other – am the first person to benefit. I believe also that if I want to forgive, then as far as you are concerned, I have already forgiven, no matter what emotional after-shocks may continue to ambush me, because forgiveness is an act of will, a decision, a choice, uniquely mine to make. It is also a grace, and I ask for it.

? *'Do you ask this of your own, or did others tell you about me?' (John 18:34)*

Pontius Pilate, the Roman procurator, had just asked you, Jesus, whether you were the king of the Jews. Your reply was, in effect, to ask him whether the question was his own or prompted by others. His response was to indicate that it was from the Jews. He showed clearly in this meeting that he did not care about issues of truth: his dismissive question, 'What is truth?' made that clear enough. He was cynical, concerned to protect his position and not allow anything to happen which might prejudice it. If he took no action when someone called himself king of the Jews he would be in trouble with the emperor. Pilate never forgot to think of Rome.

But, Jesus, you had made no claim to kingship. When others made it on your behalf, you rejected it. But Pilate, for all his preoccupation with his position, was not as shamelessly unscrupulous as the chief priests who presented the case to him as a political challenge to Roman rule, though knowing that was false. As if that were not bad enough, they went on to say, 'We have no king but the emperor,' a statement which, from them, was a denial of the covenant by which they pledged themselves to God.

This was a sordid episode of wheeling and dealing for the sake of maintaining power. Pilate's power was military, working from without, and he made an effort to save you from a verdict he knew to be unjust. The chief priests' power was spiritual, working from within, and they made every effort to have you convicted, though guiltless – while landing Pilate with the blame. They were guilty of a greater sin: the corruption of the best is the worst.

Jesus, in this episode you changed the relationship with Pilate. He began as prosecutor, demanding, 'What have you done?' but ended as defendant, washing his hands of the affair. You began as defendant, but ended by pointing to your Father as the source of all power. You turned the tables on Pilate. You did not take kindly to those who sought to reduce truth to the level of a bargaining-chip. If they were capable of it, they learned not to do that again.

Your question applies to me in another way. It asks whether I know you of myself or only at second-hand. You want my knowledge to go beyond borrowed information and come from the realm of experience. And a good way – not an easy way – for a person to grow in affinity for you, a sense of identification with you, is to share the life of the poor. I believe I will more quickly grow to know you by a little loving than by much reasoning.

Lord, the woman you spoke to was Mary Magdalene, and the time was after your resurrection. She had gone to the tomb where you had been buried and she found it empty. Thinking your body had been stolen, she was upset, and cried. But why did she look for the living among the dead? Because her faith was not yet fully alive to who you were.

Then, turning round, she saw you but did not recognise you. Clearly, in your risen form, you were different from before: resurrection was not a matter of going back to where you had left off, as if your passion and death were merely an interruption. Resurrection meant a qualitatively new kind of life.

She did not recognise you, thinking you were a gardener; there is a sense, perhaps, in which she thought you were *only* a gardener. She failed to see you in an ordinary person, as if to say, 'How could Jesus be present in anyone so run-of-the-mill?' But she missed the hint planted in her error: the garden of Gethsemane and the garden of your burial were God's response to Adam's sin in the garden of paradise, a word originally meaning a garden.

She did not recognise you until you called her by name. But once you did so, she turned and answered 'Teacher!' Where there is a greeting, there is a meeting. After your resurrection, Lord, you were seen by your disciples, not by others. It takes faith to know you as you are, and to recognise you in the mundane human beings around us, such as gardeners, carpenters and fishermen.

You said to her, 'Do not hold on to me.' Were you implying, 'Do not cling to an image of me'? Or was it more, 'Do not think you can hold on to the past. Do not try to fence me in, to contain me, to define me, to limit me'? Indeed, I cannot with truth proclaim a risen Christ as long as I cling to a past that is dead. We try to do that.

Instead, you gave Mary a mission; you sent her – an apostle to the apostles – to give the brothers your message: 'I am ascending to my Father and your Father, to my God and your God.' She did this, and her message was as simple as it was comprehensive, 'I have seen the Lord.' What more did she – or anyone – need to say? And your last word in this episode, Lord, was as always about God your Father, the one to whom your thoughts turned, especially in the key moments of your life and work. May it be so with me also.

? *'You have no fish, have you?' (John 21:4)*

This was after your resurrection, Lord. Just after daybreak, standing on the beach, you put this simplest of questions to a group of your followers who had gone fishing in a boat. It was not met with unreserved enthusiasm: the failed fishermen gave a blunt answer, 'No.' But I imagine you were glad to receive – for once – a straight answer to a straight question; that was exceptional, and therefore all the more welcome.

I wonder if the question annoyed them, just enough perhaps to arouse their curiosity as to whom this stranger might be, questioning them in the early hours of the morning after a night of failure. A buyer, perhaps? Then you prepared a charcoal fire there, with fish on it, and bread, and you said to them, 'Come and have breakfast.' If there wasn't a smile on your face, Lord, I think there was at least a twinkle in your eye.

Your question, and the actions which accompanied it, evokes memories. It recalls loaves and fishes, a message of God's overflowing generosity. It recalls your raising to life of the daughter of Jairus, when you told her parents to give her something to eat; you had a sense of the practical, the physical, the corporeal. And, like an earlier question, 'How many loaves have you?', it was a wake-up call. It is like the question, 'Have you anything here to eat?' which you put to some followers in a similar situation. And your actions on this occasion turned the disciples' no into a yes: they started with nothing but finished with everything, by doing what you told them. It was just after daybreak; was it beginning to dawn – on them?

Your question was a reality test. Indeed it was a statement more than a question. It said, 'I am here, and I am real. Come and see.' You made your reality present in a way that fishermen would understand best, that is, by giving them an abundance of fish. It is not surprising to me that early Christians took a fish as their secret symbol, the Greek word for a fish, *icthus*, being an acronym for Jesus Christ, the Son of God, the Saviour.

The disciple you loved was the first to become aware of what was happening, saying, 'It is the Lord.' Simon Peter should have been the first, since the incident was so similar to his calling by you; was he oblivious to anything but the work of the day? It was the loved one who was the first to see; that is often the way, is it not, Lord? Love sees the way, love finds a way.

? *'Do you love me?' (John 21:15, 16, 17)*

This question, Lord, you put to Peter. It was one of only two that you asked three times; the other was 'Whom are you looking for?' Your doing so was surely meant to underline its importance. However, I do not believe you put it to Peter in order to rub his nose in the memory of his three-fold denial of you; love keeps no score of wrong.

You are asking me, Lord, if I love you. What is my answer? I am a product of my time: I half-think, half-live, half-love, half-commit. I am a half-person, uncertain, cautious of totality, wary of absolutes ('extremes'). Is there anything more dead – or deadlier – than a little reasonable religion? I notice that you were sparing in your use of the word 'love'; I think you saw it as too precious to be bandied around.

I know that I cannot expect to love you as I love people. I know you and know people differently; you by faith, people by experience, different types of love. I am not aware of an emotional love for you as for family and friends. But would I obey you rather than a person I loved, if that person asked me to do something I clearly knew to be wrong? I hope I would. Religion is not reducible to morals but they are the sign of its authenticity. Is that to intellectualise away the thrust of your question? I do not think so; I think it is to give it content, because in my time the word 'love' has been emptied of content through overuse and misuse.

Love makes a person vulnerable, and that is something I fear. Love is the doorway that opens to pain, suffering and loss. Within the hardened shell of the isolated self, inside the crusty carapace of the individual, one is safe from the pain of love. Not a bad description of hell. Love is the bridge between the land of the dead and the land of the living.

To answer your question, Lord, I have to ask others: Do I love myself? If not, then I cannot love anyone else. I am aware of much in myself that is unlovable. I hesitate to soil the word 'love' by applying it to myself. I know I am self-centred and selfish, and they are a parody of love. I have the self-loathing common to our time – all times? – which debilitates and belittles, a counterfeit humility. Do I respect myself? I cannot love what I do not respect. Do I know myself? It is the beginning of all growth.

Lord, I do not want to give a facile answer to a searching question. All loves are one: to love one is to love all; not to love one is not to love any. What I do know is that I want to love; is that enough?

? *'If it is my will that he remain until I come, what is that to you?*
● *Follow me!' (John 21:23)*

Talk first and think afterwards, if at all: was that Peter's motto? He charged in, head down, asking, 'Lord, what about him?' referring to the disciple whom you loved. And you gave him your reply in the form of a question. This was a last rebuke to Peter, one of the many you gave him, he who was always trying to manage people, to organise them. You did not want him, or me, to run around trying to sort out other people's lives; I think you want me to make myself into the kind of person I think others ought to be. Your reply seems to say, firmly, even bluntly, 'What happens to him is none of your business. Concentrate on what is your business: follow me.' Were you not harsh with him, Jesus? Only a little while before, he had told you three times that he loved you; could you not have ignored his gaffe?

But you knew him better than I; you knew what he needed. Throughout your life, Lord, you were an intense person; you were driven by a sense of urgency, you were a man with a mission. You proclaimed the kingdom of God as a moment of definitive choice in which decisive action was called for. You saw it as God confronting people and demanding a response. From us, you called for commitment; you wanted people to come here and now, not later when we feel things might be better.

When you said, 'Follow me', you wanted your followers to do more than merely learn from you as a disciple from a rabbi, or to adopt your standards as a moral leader, or to imitate you in some kind of mimicry. You wanted our following of you to be a living in you, a sharing in your life, motivated and empowered by you. I could hardly live your life or exercise your mission, without – to borrow a phrase from your disciple Paul – being 'in you'.

What is this being 'in you'? It begins with you, Lord, and is a gift of yours, not an achievement of mine. You offered 'forgiveness for the past, spiritual power for the present, and hope for the future'. Self-knowledge and self-renunciation are the necessary starting-points to that commitment which you sought, and which is the heart of being 'in you'. Self-fulfilment is a result, a side-effect, and usually in a form entirely different from what I might have anticipated. If I seek it as a goal, I will be like someone trying to run up an escalator that is coming down, or like a person who does not understand that if he wishes to catch something he must first open his hand and let go. The great choice opens before me daily: to choose God or choose self. You continue to call, 'Follow me.'

? *'Why do you persecute me?' (Acts 9:4; 22:7; 26:14)*

How sad, Lord, that the last words the New Testament attributes to you, not once but in three places, are about our persecuting you. Saul, to whom you first put the question, was a Pharisee, a guardian of orthodoxy. He had turned religion into an ideology, from a way of meaning and motivation, about relationships and conscience, from a way of freeing people from what diminishes or belittles them, into a system of control. With the authority and commission of the chief priests, he had letters authorising him to arrest and imprison those who did not conform to the official line. This was in Acts, the gospel of the Holy Spirit, which marks the beginning of the church. But when he was knocked off his high horse, dropped the official stance and asked who you were, then Saul the persecutor became Paul, your witness and apostle.

Let me not – Judas-like – respond to your question by saying, 'Surely not I?' When do I persecute you? When I am not true to myself, but allow an office or a function to take me over and subsume me, or when I shrink in cowardice from new truths, or settle in laziness for half-truths, or arch in arrogance as if I had all truths.

I persecute you when I ignore the poor, walking past them heedlessly. It is the easiest of all options – doing nothing, in place of action substituting vague but uncommitted sentiment. Not to feed the poor is to starve them. How can I say the prayer you taught us, Lord, 'Give us this day our daily bread', if I do not care about those who have no bread?

I persecute you when I sell people short in any way. My relations with people are the barometer of my relations with you. You did not ask Saul, 'Why are you persecuting my followers?' but 'Why are you persecuting me?' To persecute them is to persecute you. To respect and care for them is to do likewise to you.

But, sorry, Lord, your question was why, not when. I do it because I impose the Ego, the Great I, on you, on others, and on nature. I am afraid I will lose out by giving of myself; I fear that others will take advantage of me if I am generous; I feel that I have to look after Number One, because if I do not, no one else will. If I believed myself to be loved unconditionally, none of that would matter, I would be freed from the necessity of protecting my interests. You say that God our Father does love us unconditionally. Terms and conditions do not apply. Why is it that I find that so hard to believe? What is the source of the resistance within me? I think fear is the answer to my question. Free me from fear, Lord, that I may live in your presence.

Acknowledgements

The scripture quotations contained herein are from the *New Revised Standard Version Bible: Catholic Edition* copyright 1989 by the Division of Christian Education of the National Council of the Churches of Christ in the USA. Used by permission. All rights reserved.

Exceptions to the above are:

Mark 8:36-37 and John 18:34, from the Douai edition, New York, USA, 1953, and

Proverbs 27:6: 'From one who hates, kisses are ominous', quoted under Luke 22:48, is from the *Jerusalem Bible*, published and copyright 1966, 1967 and 1968 by Darton, Longman and Todd Ltd and Doubleday & Co Inc and used by permission of the publishers.

The story about Moses, under Luke 22:27, is from Juliet Mabey (compiler), *Rumi: A Spiritual Treasury*, and is reproduced by permission of Oneworld Publications.

The prayer under Mark 15:34 is from *The Psalms: A New Translation*, Grail edition, Fontana, London, 1963, Psalm 21, vv 3, 12, 16, 18, 20:

'My God, I call by day and you give no reply; I call by night and I find no peace. Do not leave me alone in my distress; come close, there is none else to help. Parched as burnt clay is my throat, my tongue cleaves to my jaws. People stare at me and gloat. Lord, do not leave me alone'. Used by permission of HarperCollins Publishers Ltd.